IN AND OUT OF EACH OTHER'S BODIES

IN AND OUT OF EACH OTHER'S BODIES

THEORY OF MIND, EVOLUTION, TRUTH, AND THE NATURE OF THE SOCIAL

MAURICE BLOCH

Paradigm Publishers
Boulder • London

Copyright © 2013 Paradigm Publishers

Published in the United States by Paradigm Publishers, 5589 Arapahoe Avenue, Boulder, CO 80303 USA.

Paradigm Publishers is the trade name of Birkenkamp & Company, LLC, Dean Birkenkamp, President and Publisher.

Library of Congress Cataloging-in-Publication Data

Bloch, Maurice.
  In and out of each other's bodies : theory of mind, evolution, truth, and the nature of the social / Maurice Bloch.
    p. cm.
  ISBN 978-1-61205-102-4 (pbk. : alk. paper)
  1. Social interaction. 2. Philosophy of mind. 3. Anthropology.
4. Ethnology—Religious aspects. I. Title.
HM1111.B56 2012
302—dc23

                                                                    2012011086

Printed and bound in the United States of America on acid-free paper that meets the standards of the American National Standard for Permanence of Paper for Printed Library Materials.

Designed and Typeset by Straight Creek Bookmakers.

17 16 15 14 13   1 2 3 4 5

Contents

◇

Preface

This book contains a number of articles written in the last few years that have already been published, although often in places with which many anthropologists may not be familiar. Two of the articles appear for the first time in English (they were originally published in French).

The book is divided into three parts.

The first part concerns the nature of the social. It draws an important distinction between two types of social. On the one hand, there is the social understood as the flow of interaction between people; I call this the transactional (Chapter 2). On the other hand, the transactional social is contrasted with conscious, explicit representations of the social; these I call the transcendental social. I argue that the transcendental social consists of second-order phenomena created and maintained by rituals.

The transactional social is governed by norms and ways of doing things that are largely subconscious. It involves the continual mutual monitoring of each other by the members of a social group. In recent psychology, this monitoring of others is called "theory of mind," and it depends on what I term the "interpenetration" of individual humans (Chapter 1). The human transactional social differs only in degree from the social that we find in our close primate relatives such as chimpanzees; indeed, it is present in all social species in differing forms. It can be assumed that the transactional social was also a major feature of all pre-*sapiens* ancestors of modern humans and that it has been a driving evolutionary force behind the elaboration of theory of mind and of the human brain.

By contrast, the transcendental social is unique to *Homo sapiens*, and—prompted by our increasing knowledge of the major transformation known as the Upper Palaeolithic revolution—I venture to guess that it is a relatively late feature of human society.

The relationship between the transactional social and the transcendental social is a central concern of this volume. The transactional is fluid. It changes from instant to instant as social relations adapt to ever-transforming situations. However, human society is in part regulated by imaginary long-lasting entities. These include social roles such as queens, professors, or uncles that are apparently free of the moment. A defiance of time is also found in transcendental groups such as nations, clans, or castes, the imagination of which can last for very long periods of time, ignoring the fact of their ever-changing personnel and the mutability of their members' lives.

In Chapter 4 on teknonymy, I show how names that are attached to people by a variety of rituals imply roles that represent the people involved as permanent. This representation contrasts with the empirical transitory nature of their bodies and of social transactions. These names and associated transcendental roles are part of a large, explicitly evoked and more or less systematized transcendental. Such "systems" are not necessarily mutually exclusive from the perspective of the individual. In circumstances in which a person might be called by more than one type of name, it is possible for one person to "appear" in different, sometimes incompatible, transcendental systems.

The relationship between the transactional social and the transcendental social is motivated but transformational. This is because on the one hand the transcendental is based on the transactional. It relies on the fact that the barrier between the conscious and the subconscious is not sharp, but often permeable. However, in order for the transcendental to use for its own purposes the raw material that humans' dim awareness of the transactional makes available, it needs radically to transform the transactional. This transformation occurs by means of ritual. Ritual is little discussed in this volume because it has been the subject of much of my earlier work (e.g., Bloch 1986, 1989), yet it is the key mechanism for the creation of the transcendental and especially its most significant feature: the capability to create entities that appear to transcend the impermanence and fluidity of the transactional.

Many of the features of what I call the transcendental social are often attributed to religion. These features include ritual and, above all, elements that seem, from the outside, to be supernatural or at least counterintuitive. For instance, the capability of a nation to last for centuries while the lives of its members do not involves a feat of imagination that could be considered "religious" because it is counterintuitive. Observations of this kind form the basis of the argument in Chapter 2. There I argue that, disregarding the exceptional circumstances that gave rise to the Abrahamic religions, no valid theoretical distinction can be made between the transcendental social and the "religious." The usual uses of the word "religious" are *misleading* because they imply Western ideas about religion that are necessarily tied to the Abrahamic religions, especially Christianity. This is why I argue in Chapter 3 that when we try to imagine what life would have been like in an early Neolithic site such as Çatalhöyük in Anatolia, looking for signs of religion will inevitably confuse the issue. Instead, we should think outside the box created by the historical specificities of the Abrahamic religions, which are relative latecomers on the human scene and therefore likely to hinder the elaboration of theoretical insights into the nature of humankind.

The second part of this book (Chapters 5 and 6) concerns the ethnography of truth, by which I mean the study of the criteria and the concepts that ordinary people hold concerning what is true and why. For these two chapters, I draw on my ethnographic knowledge of the Zafimaniry people of Madagascar with whom I have been working for nearly forty years. However, I strongly believe that social anthropology ought not to limit itself to ethnography; the study of any particular case should always be linked to more general anthropological questions, in this case to questions concerning the nature of folk epistemics. Thus, in Chapter 3 on truth and sight I discuss why the sense of sight should be so regularly seen as the most veridical in cultures around the world. I argue that sight is believed to be necessarily true because it is not socially mediated, whereas hearing is linked to language that is associated with lying and the possibility of being intentionally misled by others. Chapter 6 concerns

the presence of doubt within the flow of an ordinary con-
versation. Again it is ethnographically based. I distinguish
between two types of doubt—one that appears to be temporary, the other permanent—and show how they relate to
different rhetorics of truth.

The third and final part of the book consists of two lectures given in different places and at different times. Both
help to situate my work within a more general theoretical
framework and indicate the directions I want anthropology
to take. Chapter 7 is the English translation of the inaugural
lecture I gave in 2006 for the European Chair at the Collège
de France. In such an august institution, an inaugural lecture is a formal affair delivered in front of a large audience.
As a result, the style of presentation is rather different from
the more mundane way I normally speak and write. Quite
naturally, the lecturer is expected to mention past and
present professors at the college who have influenced his
or her work. Moreover, it is conventional for the speaker to
indicate the theories and topics he or she intends to address
in subsequent lectures, thus defining the future direction of
his or her research. Chapter 8, in contrast, is not focused on
my own work, but instead is intended as an introduction to
the work of Claude Lévi-Strauss. Jointly sponsored by the
French Embassy in India and the Delhi School of Economics,
the lecture was given in New Delhi in 2008 as part of a celebration of Lévi-Strauss's one-hundredth birthday. However,
although it offers a special reading of the scholarship of the
great French anthropologist, the lecture is also relevant for
my own work—not only because I have at times been directly
influenced by Lévi-Strauss but also because a discussion of
his work, its strengths and its shortcomings, gave me the
opportunity to reflect again on the kind of direction that I
think it would be fruitful for anthropology to take.

References

Bloch, M. 1986. *From blessing to violence: History and ideology in
the circumcision ritual of the Merina of Madagascar.* Cambridge:
Cambridge University Press.
———. 1989. *Ritual, history, and power: Selected papers in anthropology.* London: Athlone Press.

1

Durkheimian Anthropology and Religion

Going In and Out of Each Other's Bodies[1]

In memory of Skip Rappaport

Emile Durkheim's work has always been criticized for rei-fying the social and situating it in an indeterminate zone between actors' consciousness and positive facts. In this chapter, however, I am not concerned with exploring whether this criticism of the founder of French sociology's work is justified. My purpose instead is to show that it is possible to retain some aspects of Durkheim's conclusions about the nature of religion and of the social with types of argument quite different from those he employed. My framework here is that of modern evolutionary natural science and recent understandings of the specificities of the human mind/brain.

Such an evolutionist perspective tends to make social/ cultural anthropologists uncomfortable. I hope that as they read on, they discover that an evolutionist perspective does not necessarily lead to the dangers they envision; and that it can even be reconciled with some of their most cherished ideas that will emerge all the stronger as a result.

But because one might as well hang for a sheep as for a lamb, I begin my argument much further back than is usual in evolutionary anthropology with a consideration of the very earliest stages of life on earth, when unicellular

1

organisms associated together to form multicellular units in the Cambrian era.

During this crucial transition, and for millions of years, it was far from clear whether those early multicellular organisms were one or many because they were in an in-between stage. This biological conundrum still exists, in varying ways and to varying degrees, for many subsequent and more complex forms of life. An extreme example is coral, about which one can argue equally plausibly either that the minute units of which it consists are separate organisms or that whole coral branches (or even whole reefs) are one single animal.

The difficulty of isolating the "individual" does not only apply for such exceptional life forms. The issue of identifying the specific unit on which natural selection acts arises in respect of all living things and has become particularly acute in modern biology. Does natural selection occur at the gene level or on combinations of associated genes? Or is it at the level of the individual? Or on a larger group that shares genes to differing degrees (Stotz and Griffiths 2004)?

This sort of question is particularly problematic when we are dealing with social species. Is it the bee or the hive that is the animal? After all, the bees in a hive are as genetically identical as are the different bits of the human body, and a hive possesses only one set of working reproductive organs.

The biological problems do not end there. When does an embryo become separate from its mother? Is a live spermatozoid a unit? More generally, how far are parents one with their children, and are descendants of individuals their continuation or new units? Are descent groups one body? Do members of one caste have unique distinctive types of blood? Are nations one people? Are we all the *children* of God in the *brotherhood* of Christ? Is society, as Durkheim claimed, more than the sum of the constituent individuals?

Here, those readers who have already given me up as some sort of biological reductionist, indifferent to the higher purpose of cultural anthropology, might summon a flicker of interest with these more familiar disciplinary questions. They may even begin to hope that I might have something to say about religion and ritual, which, after all, is what this book is about. I shall get there ... eventually. And indeed, my prime purpose in this chapter is to consider the theoretical implications of the way I have just managed to *slither* from a discussion of the structure of coral to hoary classical subjects in anthropology and even to central tenets of some interpretations of the Christian religion.

If the reader is totally unsympathetic to the approach, however, I propose they will already have revelled in identifying a familiar sleight of hand: representing facts about the world as if they were just that, without having first recited the anthropologists' exorcism prayer.

> I humbly acknowledge that everything I say is nothing but an epiphenomenon of my present cultural position and time and that this inevitably leads me to essentialize a particular cultural position and then mercilessly impose it on defenseless people.

In other words, I have been guilty of suggesting that *my* scientific knowledge, a mere elitist manifestation of my own culture, is somehow the basis of the propositions made by those people around the world who say things like this: "The members of our group, which has existed since the beginning of time, share a distinctive type of bone"; or "Our lineage consists of one body"; or "Initiation reunites us with our ancestors"; or "Ask not for whom the bell tolls; it tolls for thee."

I would have thus committed all the category mistakes in the book. Especially in having forgotten the fact that the cultural creates an impenetrable screen between what is and our cultural representations. Familiar arguments of this kind might be partly justified as first steps when we teach an introduction to anthropology,[2] but in this chapter I argue that when left in categorical form, they are as misleading as the ethnocentricism that anthropologists love to denounce.

We can start with a classic and familiar polemic as a way of introducing the theoretical position I shall adopt here.

In the bad old days, so the story goes, anthropologists used to think that kinship was based on the fact that people go in and out of each other's bodies. Indeed, they might have stressed that the physical separation of a child from its mother takes quite a while, with intermediate phases such as breast feeding and child care. Some of these earlier vulgar anthropologists went as far as to suggest that the care given by fathers to infants was somehow the consequence of having gone into the mother during sexual intercourse. They argued that these "natural" foundations were the common base of all different kinship systems (Yanagisako and Collier 1987, 30–35).

Such naïveté, however, was soon to be severely disciplined by developments in our subject. First, anthropologists stressed the old platonic point that humans do not live in the world as God or the scientists see it, but *via* their own understanding of it (I don't see why this does not apply to other animals, too). From this they argued that *the foundation* (i.e., going in and out of each other's bodies) cannot be the direct foundation of social knowledge. This correction was, however, soon deemed not to have been severe enough. It was not simply that people saw the world "through a glass darkly"; it was that they did not see it at all. There was no such *fact* as that people went in and out of each other's bodies; they were just accidental cultural representations of which my particular formulation is only one among many. Thus, to talk of different, culturally constructed kinship systems as if they were cultural interpretations of a single reality was a fallacy. In a wonderful metaphor, David Schneider explained that if you went out into the world armed with a kinship-shaped cutting tool, you inevitably got kinship-shaped pieces. By this he implied that if the tool had had any other shape than the western–shaped kinship tool, which would be the case with the tools used by the "others," you would have gotten a quite different shape (Schneider 1984, 198).

I have always liked this metaphor of Schneider's because, as a child, I used to spend much time watching my grandmother making biscuits. She would roll out a large flat pancake of dough on the marble of the kitchen table, and with a few ancient tin tools she would cut out various shapes. This is exactly what Schneider has in mind. But the other reason why I like his metaphor is that what is wrong with it is also obvious. The world in which people go in and out of each other, the denounced *foundation,* is not (as Schneider's analogy suggests) inert, undifferentiated, and flat like biscuit dough. It has a shape, and this shape, while it does not determine the way the world will be represented, severely restricts the parameters of what is likely.

Plato also used a culinary metaphor to talk about the world. For him, however, the world was more like a roast chicken than pastry, and unless you really wanted to make things difficult for yourself, you would "carve it at the joints," wherever they occurred on the animal you were serving up.

Indeed, it is the dialectic between the facts of sex and birth and the cultural representations of these phenomena that most promises to advance our understanding of the nature of human beings, which, of course also involves the cultural (and hence historical) aspect. But examination of this dialectic is what the Schneiderian rhetoric makes impossible by refusing to allow us to ask what the representations "are about" and what the world is like. A trivial objection to the effect that not all languages have a word for what anthropologists call "kinship" puts a stop to any consideration of the really important questions about our species.

And there is yet something else that is obscured by Schneider's figure of speech. The cutting tools, which represent concepts in the metaphor, also have to be explained. There is no doubt that these tools are the products of specific histories but they nevertheless have had to be usable by the minds of the human beings who employ them. Here again, the world interacts in a challenging way with the representations that cultural anthropologists study. It is banal to stress merely that the world we live in is culturally constructed; what is of interest is the indirect relation of the construction to what is constructed and how the construction is used.

This chapter, however, will not pursue the implications of the link between the fact that we go in and out of each other's bodies in birth and sex and the cultural representations of this fact in kinship systems. Many (I do not include myself among them) might feel that this topic has grown tiresome. I merely evoke the controversy to stress that because all cultures interpret, and have to interpret, the fact that we go in and out of each other in sex and birth, they also have to interpret the consequent fact that for us (as with coral) there is indeterminacy concerning the physical boundaries of individuals. For instance, the so-called "descent theorists" of my anthropological youth were fascinated with groups of people who declare themselves to be "one body"; in other words, corporate groups. These statements are interesting not because they are flights of fancy proving yet again that the world we live in is culturally constructed but because they are in part motivated by the very real fact of the indeterminacy and arbitrariness of the boundaries of biological units.

My focus in this chapter concerns another real fact about human beings that, although it concerns a matter different from kinship, is not altogether unrelated to it. Indeterminacy and arbitrariness of boundaries are not simply the result of the sexual character of our species and the way it reproduces itself. They are also due to another feature of *Homo sapiens*. Individuals go in and out of each other because of certain characteristics of the human nervous system. This form of interpenetration is as material as sex and birth; but unlike sex and birth it is more or less unique to our species (Povinelli et al. 2000; Decety and Somerville 2003).

I have already mentioned that, although the boundaries of individual units are arbitrary among all living forms, this ambiguity takes on a special, perhaps more extreme form in social animals because the social—of itself and by definition—continually reconnects the individuals whom time and genealogical distance are separating. Such a process occurs in a variety of ways in different life forms because of the mechanisms that make the social differ according to the species concerned. So it is not surprising that the specific basis of human sociability is a product of those capacities of our species that make it distinctive (Humphrey 2002).

One thing that normal human babies do at about 1 year old, but our nearest relatives, the chimpanzees, never do, is point at things, not because they want what they designate—they do this, but so do chimps—but because they want the people around them to pay attention to the same things. In other words, they want the people they are with to adjust their minds in harmony with theirs—in short, to share intentionality (Gopnik 1993; Tomasello and Rakoczy 2003; Tomasello 1999). This demonstrative pointing is one of the first stages of the development of that unique and probably most important of human capacities: the ability to "read" the mind of others, a capacity that is somewhat oddly referred to as "theory of mind" (TOM for short). This ability continues to develop from the age of 12 months on until the child reaches the age when it can be shown that the child "knows" that other people act in terms of the beliefs or concepts they hold, rather than in terms of how the world is (Wimmer and Perner 1983). By "know," I simply mean that the child and, of course, the adult, acts in terms of their reading of the beliefs of *alter* and continually adjusts her behavior accordingly. I do not mean that the person who does this is necessarily conscious of the process (a point to which I shall return in a moment). The whole process is far too complex and too rapid for that to be possible. Nonetheless, the importance of TOM can hardly be overestimated. Those familiar with Gricean theories of linguistic pragmatics will realize that it can be argued, convincingly in my opinion, that this continual mind reading is what makes linguistic communication, and indeed all complex human communication, possible (Sperber and Wilson 1986).

It is legitimate to think that to talk of the mutual mind reading on which our social life is based is, at best, simply a metaphor; at worst, a mystification. However, I want to stress that the metaphor refers to an empirical phenomenon of interpenetration, even though admittedly we don't stick our finger into each other's brains in some kind of mental intercourse.

Just how material the process of mind reading may be has become clearer in the light of recent neurological findings. For instance, many researchers now argue that the unique human ability to read the mind of those with whom we interact is ultimately based on a much more general feature of the brain that is not confined to humans: the so-called "mirror neurones" (Gallese and Goldman 1998).

Perhaps the term is misleading. What is being referred to is an observation that has been made possible by modern neural imagery. The term *mirror neurones* means that exactly the same neurones are activated in our brains when, for example, we see someone raising their arm to point at the ceiling as when we perform the action ourselves. In other words, the action of *alter* requires from us a part of the same physiological process: the neural part as the action of *ego*. Indeed, a moment's reflection makes us realize that, even without the arcane and somewhat contested biology of mirror neurones, the very nature of human communication *must* involve something like this (Decety and Somerville 2003).[3]

Let us consider a simple act of linguistic communication. Here I follow Sperber and Wilson's theory of relevance fairly closely (Sperber and Wilson 1986). For my message to come across when I say, for example: "Today we honor the memory of Roy Rappaport" a mechanism must occur that enables you to penetrate my brain and align yours so that its neuronal organization resembles mine. In order to do this, we both had to use a tool, sound waves in this case, but it cannot possibly be the sound waves, as such, that carried my meaning to you. Sound waves, poor things, are just sound waves. The reality is that sound waves enable me to modify your brain, or mind, so that its neuronal organization in part resembles mine, admittedly in a very limited way. And, of course, the ability to communicate in this way—to connect our neurones—is what makes culture possible because culture must ultimately be based on the exchange of information. This can then be combined with other information and then transformed or reproduced through time and across space in a uniquely human way.

The parallel neuronal modification implied by communication has further important implications. Let us assume, for the sake of argument, that it is possible for an individual to create ex nihilo a representation. Such a representation could then be said to be under that individual's control because the process that produced it would be hers alone. However, when the representation comes from someone else's brain (i.e., when it comes *via* the process of communication, which is in fact always the case, though to varying extents), the representation of one brain colonizes another. This process, whether it is conscious or subconscious, is the basis of all communication. In such a case, the created neuronal activity of one brain *is* the material existing in another. By this means, the brains of different individuals interpenetrate materially so that the boundaries that we believe to be obvious become problematic. What I am saying is very similar to what some writers, especially Ed Hutchins, call "distributed cognition" (Hutchins 1995). However, I would distance my argument from them on one minor point. Hutchins, in talking about this phenomenon, likes to refer to minds "not bounded by the skin" as if some sort of extra-biological process existed. I am too literal-minded to feel comfortable with such phraseology, which makes the process in question appear surreal. The process of interpenetration I am discussing is straightforward and biological.

My other difference from the distributed cognition folks is not a disagreement; I simply would like to push their insights further. Hutchins is famous for his demonstration of the way the knowledge necessary to navigate a big ship is not held in the head of any one crew member; it is distributed in a group. In an action such as coping with an emergency, each individual does his job as best he can in the light of his own knowledge, but in doing so he relies on other individuals who have other bits of knowledge necessary to navigate the ship that he does not and does not need to have. This is what Hutchins calls distributed cognition. For this type of reliance on the knowledge of others to be possible, the different individuals need to trust that the others know what they are doing and are well intentioned. This means that people can then act on what they know is incomplete knowledge, but which they trust is completed by the knowledge others have, to the extent of acting on that which they do not need fully to understand. It is not that they rely wholly on others; they rely on others at the very moment they rely on their own knowledge.

By using this particular formulation, I deliberately align what I am saying with the point made by a group of philosophers who, following Hilary Putnam and the "deference" theorists, stress that social life is based on trust of others; basically on the default assumption that these others with whom we are in contact are normally competent and cooperative. In other words, because of our theory of mind adaptation, we continually interpenetrate as we communicate and hold as true information that makes sense only because it is also contained or continuous with that in other minds (Putnam 1975; Burge 1993; Orrigi 2000). This is the nature of human cognition, which is essentially social. Such a state of affairs makes it possible that the content of knowledge stored in an individual is not to be understood nor consciously sought to be understood, but this individual is likely to be aware of the solidarity on which the whole system of social cognition is based, and this may be greatly valued. This is a point to which I shall return.

* * *

I started this chapter by arguing that for all living things, humans included, the distinctness of the units of life is far from clear. Furthermore, I argued that for people this fact is commonly represented in the kinship systems that are *about* this reality in culturally varied and specific ways. For social animals the problem of the blurring of individual boundaries is compounded by the very nature of their sociality. Individuals in social species are, to varying degrees, materially continuous with each other. Because humans are social animals, this problem applies to them. In their case, this state of affairs is brought about by the tool that makes human sociability possible: the hard-wired human capacity referred to as theory of mind. Such an assertion, however, raises the same question that I touched on in the discussion of sex and birth: What are the cultural implications, if any, of this fact? The necessity to ask this difficult question is precisely what is missing from much of the work of evolutionists such as Tooby and Cosmides (Cosmides and Tooby 1992) and even Rappaport.

The parallel with kinship may help to advance the argument, but at the same time it highlights an obvious difficulty. When anthropologists study kinship systems, they are studying representations of phenomena having to do with obvious empirical processes, of which no one can be unaware: going in and out of each other's bodies. When we examine the interpenetrations of minds, however, we are dealing with phenomena not so easily consciously perceived. The continual mutual reading of minds on which communication depends is like grammar: it is and has to be subconscious, if only to operate at the necessary speed. But, if that is so, how is it possible that an *awareness* of this process could occur, a necessary step for it to take explicit form in cultural representations? To approach this question, I ask the reader to accompany me on a detour, away from purely theoretical considerations and toward a brief description of an empirical case.

About a year ago, I decided to do a new (for me) type of field research in the remote Malagasy forest village in which I have been working on and off for nearly 40 years. I carried out what is probably the most typical experiment used to demonstrate the development of children's understanding of TOM in front of any villagers who were available at the time; I then asked the adults watching to make sense of what they had just seen. By inviting them to give me *their* interpretation of what was going on, I placed my informants in the same situation as that in which professional psychologists normally find themselves in the lab. The experiment in question is usually called the "false belief task." In the version I used, I showed a child two hats, and I placed sweets under one of them in the front of the child and everyone else present. I then asked a member of the audience to leave the house and, showing the child what I was doing, I switched the treasure to the other hat. I then asked the child—this is the key question—under which hat the person who had just gone out of the house would look for the sweets when they returned. The results in the Malagasy village were, as expected, much the same as those reported from all over the world. Younger children say that the person who left the house will look under the hat where the sweets actually are, while older children say that the person will look under the hat where he or she saw them put, but where, of course, they no longer are. This difference is usually interpreted by psychologists to mean that the younger child has not yet subconsciously understood that other people do not necessarily know what they know. To put it more theoretically and somewhat differently, the younger child has not yet subconsciously understood that people act in terms of their possibly false beliefs, not in terms of what the world is actually like.

The adult Malagasy villagers' interpretation of the experiment was not all that different from that of professional cognitive psychologists. After a bit of prodding and reflection, the commonest explanation was that younger children have not yet learned to lie, so they do not understand that other people can also lie. For reasons that I cannot go into here, I take this to mean that the younger children are represented by them as naïve empiricists, while they believe the older children and adults know that people can deceive and therefore look for the communicative *intention* of the speaker because they do not simply trust appearances that could be manipulated by people.

I then used the discussion of the results of this experiment, which had been conducted in front of villagers, as a springboard for a more general discussion about the nature of thought. During these continuing discussions, the villagers explained that thought was an activity through which one matched one's action to one's purpose. Thought, they reasoned, is thus a feature of all animals. Fleas, for example, also think because they hide in the seams of garments in order not to get caught. Humans, however, are superior to other animals in that they have an extra tool—language—that enables them to achieve the purpose of their thought more efficiently especially through indirectness and deceit.

When I consider the very detailed information on mind, thought, and cognitive development that I obtained through this work from the largely unschooled Malagasy in this remote village, I am, above all, struck by the familiarity of the ideas they expressed and their similarity with our own folk view. I am also impressed by the correspondence between their views and those of the psychologists. And, indeed, when I look at the few other ethnographic studies of folk theories of mind and thought we possess, I find this general family likeness again and again (Gubser 1965; Rosaldo 1980).[4]

These similarities inevitably raise the question of what causes such recurrences. The obvious answer is that they are triggered by an awareness of the same actual universal human cognitive process. This explanation, however, runs into the difficulty discussed previously, that mental processes such as the workings of the mind operate below the level of consciousness while what I was told in the discussions that followed the experiments was clearly explicit and conscious.

But is this difficulty as serious as it seems? Or, to put it another way, following the arguments of a number of cognitive scientists (Jackendoff 1987; Block 1993; Humphrey 2002), is the barrier between the conscious and the subconscious as impenetrable as the objection assumes? The comparison with grammar, alluded to previously, suggests otherwise. When we speak to or comprehend others, we do not consciously obey grammatical rules; nevertheless, we can *become* aware of the existence of such rules when, for example, somebody makes a "grammatical" mistake. Indeed, it is probably as a result of such "mistakes" that folk grammarians the world over can build their theories. Although these folk grammatical theories vary probably because of a great variety of historical and cultural factors, it would surely be perverse not to accept that their obvious similarities are caused by the way grammar actually works and that this can be accessed to a degree.

The situation with theory of mind is probably similar, perhaps also based on reflection prompted by instances of faulty or difficult communication. For example, much of the general speculation about the nature of mind and thought in the data I collected in the Malagasy village was linked to explicit reflection on the abilities and limitations of a co-resident deaf and dumb man. It seems that this sort of more familiar and recurrent event causes the same kind of continual attempt to understand the psychology of thought and communication as was artificially stimulated by my experiment. This is probably why villagers were so willing, enthusiastic even, to engage in the discussion of the experiment I had conducted once their initial resistance was overcome. The intellectual challenge it presented was not as unusual or bizarre as it might at first seem from the outside. Of course, this more ordinary speculation was not done in the jargon of modern psychology, but with the cultural tools available. But even these unsophisticated tools and vocabulary must have been developed in relation to psychological processes that actually occur and are known to occur. It is not surprising, therefore, that similar ideas and representations should crop up, again and again, in different cultural and historical contexts. In making this claim, I am not arguing for any direct determinism between the actual working of the mind and people's theories about it. Many other factors are clearly involved in each case. The working of the mind is difficult for the Malagasy to understand and represent, as indeed it is for any psychologist. It involves peeping past barriers of many kinds by means of thought or practical experiments, but both parties do this and for neither party is this completely impossible.

To illustrate such complexity and to begin to approach the subject of religion and ritual, I return to my case study.

When the Malagasy villagers so emphatically insisted that thought always, directly or indirectly, was a matter of matching ends and means, I was naturally led to ask them about dreams. Were these not a case of thought without a practical end in view? The commonest answer I was given to such a question was negative. Dreams, I was assured, occurred when other people entered you and thought *through* you in order to achieve their ends. In this way, local cognitive theory was made coherent with a theory of interpenetration with which I had become familiar when I studied Malagasy ancestor worship. This is because it is through dreams that ancestors manifest themselves most typically, and make their desires known.

This local theory of dreams is radically different from what is found in many other cultures, including that of professional psychologists. This, however, does not mean that as soon as we touch on phenomena that are usually labeled religious, we inevitably move away from concerns cognate with those of professional cognitive science. The idea that dreams are really other people, especially ancestors, thinking through you for their own ends is part of that much more general idea that previous generations, dead forebears, living elders, or absent members of the family are speaking through you as you consciously or subconsciously "quote" them. Not only are you expected to utter the words of other wise people because you trust and rely on them. But a person's forebears are thought to be continually acting through him or her. Indeed, to allow that to happen willingly is to show respect and to act morally. Morality is thus experienced, less as a matter of individual choice and more as a matter of submission and recognition of the presence of others who penetrate you. As soon as we rephrase the Malagasy concept of ancestors in this (to my mind) ethnographically more accurate way, we find that we have returned to the familiar territory of scientific theories of distributed cognition and deference mentioned previously. In the very area in which my Malagasy co-villagers could be represented as most exotic—notably their beliefs in the power of ancestors—we find them very close to Hutchins and Putnam. Even their belief in the penetration of the young by elders and ancestors turns out to be built on an implicit recognition of the effect of interpenetration made possible by TOM—on the real fact that knowledge is distributed.

The point I want to stress is that the operation of theory of mind and the nature of the distribution of knowledge in society are neither unknown nor fully known by the Malagasy villagers I studied. Furthermore, they are aware of the unsatisfactory partial nature of their knowledge, often commenting on this during the discussions that followed the experiments. And, as a result of their realization of the incompleteness of their knowledge, when the chance arises, as when I showed them the false belief task or when they observed the deaf and dumb man, they eagerly seize the opportunity to find out more about their own and others' mental processes. In that inquisitiveness they are no different from professional scientists. Like them, their knowledge is incomplete, but also like them they *strain* to know more about a reality that, in the case of psychological processes, is common to all human beings and partly accessible. Of course, as in the case of the scientists, but probably to a greater extent, there are many other factors that interact with the villagers' theoretical speculation and representations, and this multiplicity of factors produces systems that are only partly scientifically motivated. However, it is the commonality of the enterprises and the reality of the world they engage with that explains the continuity between scientific discussion of such things as theory of mind and the cultural representations of largely unschooled Malagasy villagers and Western scientists.

The bodily interpenetration of TOM is thus, to a certain degree, known by Malagasy villagers, and this knowledge combines in varying ways and in varying contexts with other types of knowledge. This leads to partial continuities between scientific and folk understandings of the interpenetration of individuals and of the consequent provisionality of levels of individuation. It is to these that I now turn.

A central implication of TOM is that all social relation implies interpenetration, so the arbitrariness of boundaries within the social fabric applies not just to people who are related but also between all human beings who are in contact. Awareness of this ensures that ideologies of individualism are always, to varying degrees, negated by ideologies based on the realisation of interconnection, as Mauss stressed in his seminal essay on the gift (Mauss 1923–1924).

Knowledge of interpenetration and of the lack of clear boundaries, as well as the emotions that are an integral element of the way these phenomena are experienced, is what is meant by that most Durkheimian of words: *solidarity*. The presence of this sentiment, at its most general, is one that is difficult to put one's finger on, because it seems rarely made explicit or the subject of reflexive discourse. However, from my reading of ethnography and from my own experience, it would seem that a default assumption in most cultures is that there is a potential moral obligation to any stranger with whom one might come into contact or, to put it in a different way, that the very fact of entering into a relationship implies being consubstantial and therefore morally obligated. Perhaps the most familiar manifestation of this phenomenon is the obligation of hospitality toward strangers, a moral imperative that recurs, admittedly in different forms, in so many unrelated cultures but that, as far as I know, has been little theorized at a comparative level by modern anthropologists. This general unspecific morality is probably an epiphenomenon of the very nature of human communication.

There are, however, many instances of much more specific and elaborate awareness of the lack of boundary between individuals. Many of them seem to fall in the domain that is usually labeled as religion, though some are of a less amiable and more threatening form. I have already mentioned the Malagasy interpretation of dreams and its link with ancestor worship. Ancestor worship is found all over the world in a variety of forms and is often linked to the lack of bodily differentiation within descent groups. Other examples are witchcraft-like ideas that often take the form of a belief in the secret and evil penetration of one's body by a consuming other made possible by the existence of communication. More obvious still are beliefs in spirit possession that seem to crop up all over the world. These beliefs are an extreme representation of the colonizing nature of social relations because they involve the total invasion and replacement of one individual's intentional mind by that of another.

In a somewhat different way, the realization of the interpenetration of individuals and of the context dependence of boundaries also seems present in many political movements and religions. The idea of a corporal unity beyond the individual is well documented for certain forms of Christianity, Islam, and devotional Hinduism. They emphasize an alternative "brotherhood" to that based on interpenetration of sex and birth, thereby highlighting the comparability of the two types of interpenetration at the same time as using the one to challenge the other. These ideas become most explicit in the mystical forms of these religions, for example in Sufism or devotional Hinduism, in which the theme of the interpenetration of the bodies of the devotees and the lack of boundaries of their bodies takes an extreme and dramatic form.

Perhaps, however, it is in ritual that the conscious and culturally encoded awareness of lack of boundedness is clearest. This, of course, was one of Durkheim's key points, but what he stressed was the effervescence of highly dramatic rituals.

There is no doubt that feelings of transcendence of individuality and even of dissolution of self into a greater whole occur in many of the manifestations that we would label as ritual. Furthermore, these may well be part of the realization of the empirical lack of boundary of human individuals. However, many rituals are simply not like that. One universal feature of ritual, however, is deference, if only because it is at the very core of the meaning of the English term. Deference is, as noted previously, the acceptance of the content of other minds without necessarily knowing the whys and wherefores of the propositions and actions one performs. As argued in different ways by Putnam, Burge, and Hutchins, this is characteristic of knowledge in society and implies cognitive interpenetration. Ritual is an extreme case of this. In ritual one accepts that the motivation for meaning is to be found in others one trusts (Bloch 2004). In other words, it is not only that one surrenders one's intentionality to others but also that one is aware of this happening. Recourse to ritual is therefore to be understood not only as awareness of neural interpenetration, a submission to other minds, but also as a celebration of such awareness.

Of course, religious and ritual representations are not simply realizations of the fact that we interpenetrate each other as we interact and that the boundaries separating individuals are provisional and alterable. In each and every case, much more is involved that might indeed be more important in the particular case. I am simply saying that the social, sexual, and reproductive characteristics of the human species means that we go in and out of each other's bodies in at least three different ways, and that this implies an indeterminacy of the level of relevant differentiation. In the case of birth and sex, the interpenetration is inevitably, though variously, cognized. In the case of TOM, the matter is more complicated, however. The working of TOM is normally below consciousness as is also the interpenetration it involves. However, because the boundary between the conscious and the subconscious is not sharp and because we have tools to traverse it (such as experiments or the existence of deaf and dumb relatives), we can use our hazy awareness of the process to interpret and speculate about such phenomena as dreams, the relation with ancestors, and many other central aspects of human life. This knowledge—the raw material of interpenetration—

becomes a resource and an idiom that can become central in many representations that we would label as moral, religious, or ritual. It is this line of causation from the fact of interpenetration to its conscious representations by different people in different ways that makes it possible to *slither* from the biological to the cultural, including the religious.

In so far as this causal chain involves a direct connection between the social, the moral, the religious, and ritual, such an argument is inevitably reminiscent of Durkheim's theories. After all, the central argument of *The Elementary Forms of the Religious Life* is that religion, by means of ritual, is a projection of the intuition of the dependence of the individual on society, and of the individual's incompleteness—an intuition that gives rise to the impression of the presence of a superior transcendental element: the religious (Durkheim 1912).

My admiration for this great anthropologist cannot but be heightened by the similarity of our arguments. Much of what I have said is what he said long ago, though from a totally different epistemological base. For this reason, it is also essential to stress the profound difference between his argument and my own, if only to clarify the status of what I have been arguing.

Unlike Durkheim, I am not proposing a general theory of "religion." Like most modern anthropologists, I do not believe that the term *religion* has any general analytical value. To seek the essence of religion would, therefore, inevitably run into the circularity for which *The Elementary Forms of the Religious Life* has been criticized. In any case, awareness of the provisional nature of individual boundaries occurs in many kinds of cultural representations that could never reasonably be termed religious. For the same reason, I am not arguing that the interpenetrations of kinship and TOM are the *origin* of the religious; any such claim would be meaningless because for me what anthropologists call *religion* is merely a ragbag of loosely connected elements without a common core.

Most importantly, however, I differ from Durkheim in his understanding of causation. For Durkheim the social, which comes from we know not where, mysteriously causes the cultural, which then gives us the tools to invent what is, irrespective of what the world is like. This idealist fantasy would be worth elaborating only as a quaint example of an archaic conceit if it did not in my opinion still resemble much contemporary anthropological theorizing.

What I am proposing is more straightforward, more modest, more materialist, and anchored in evolutionary theory. The source of the social is to be found in the cognitive capacities of humans, though, of course, the evolutionary line of causation between the social and the cognitive is not unidirectional but rather, as argued by Humphrey and Tomasello, a single process. This socio/cognitive means that, even more than is the case for nonsocial animals and differently from the case for other social animals, the boundaries between human individuals are partial at best. This fact and our consequent bodily connectedness, which supplements and sometimes competes with the connectedness of kinship, are fuzzily available to our consciousness. It is this awareness that becomes a recurrent element in a great variety of representations in different cultures, representations that we must not forget are different kinds of phenomena from the simply psychological. It is these kinds of awareness that Durkheim examined under the label "solidarity." And, furthermore, the types of solidarity he identified are often, though not always (as he also stressed) manifest in what we call religion and ritual.

Notes

1. An earlier version of this was given to the American Association for the Anthropology of Religion as a Rappoport lecture. I would like to thank R. Astuti, E. Keller, G. Orrigi, A. Yengoyan, and D. Sperber for comments on an earlier version.

2. They are what would be used to dismiss as irrelevant studies such as those of Cosmides and Tooby (1992) about cheater detection.

3. It is also important to remember the importance of sharing of emotions, which is highly relevant to the argument of this chapter and goes in the same direction as the evidence on TOM. It is not considered here, but I hope to do so in another publication. See de Waal 1996.

4. Rosaldo's book, in fact, emphasizes the exotic character of Ilongot psychology, but I am struck that, in matters of cognition at least, Ilongot conceptualization is very familiar.

References

Bloch, M. 2004. Ritual and deference. In *Ritual and memory: Toward a comparative anthropology of religion* (eds) H. Whitehouse and J. Laidlaw, 65–78. Walnut Creek, CA: Altamira Press.

Block, N. 1993. The computer model of the mind. In *Readings in philosophy and cognitive science* (ed) A. Goldman, 819–832. Cambridge, MA: MIT Press.

Burge, T. 1993. Content preservation. *The Philosophical Review* 102, 457–488.

Cosmides, L., and J. Tooby. 1992. Cognitive adaptation for social exchange. In *The adapted mind: Evolutionary psychology and the generation of culture* (eds) J. H. Barkow, L. Cosmides, and J. Tooby, 163–228. Oxford: Oxford University Press.

Decety, J., and J. A. Somerville. 2003. Shared representations between self and other: A social cognitive neuroscience view. *Trends in Cognitive Sciences* 7, 527–533.

de Waal, F. B. M. 1996. *Good natured: The origins of right and wrong in humans and other animals.* Cambridge, MA: Harvard University Press.

Durkheim, E. 1912. *Les formes élémentaires de la vie religieuse.* Paris: Alcan. (Translated 1915. *The elementary forms of the religious life.* London: Allen Unwin).

Gallese, V., and A. Goldman. 1998. Mirror neurones and the simulation theory of mind. *Trends in Cognitive Science* 12, 493–501.

Gopnik, A. 1993. How we know our minds: The illusion of first person knowledge of intentionality. *Behavioural and Brain Science* 1, 90–101.

Gubser, N. 1965. *The Nunamiut Eskimos: Hunters of caribou.* New Haven, CT: Yale University Press.

Humphrey, N. 2002. *The mind made flesh: Essays from the frontiers of psychology and evolution.* Oxford: Oxford University Press.

Hutchins, E. 1995. *Cognition in the wild.* Cambridge, MA: MIT Press.

Jackendoff, R. 1987. *Consciousness and the computational mind.* Cambridge, MA: MIT Press.

Mauss, M. 1923–1924. Essai sur le don: Forme et raison de l'échange dans les sociétés archaïques. *L'Année Sociologique,* seconde série, 30–186.

Origgi, G. 2000. Croire sans comprendre. *Cahiers de philosophie de l'Université de Caen,* 34, 191–201.

Povinelli, D. J., J. M. Bering, and S. Giambrone. 2000. Towards a science of other minds: Escaping the arguments by analogy. *Cognitive Science* 24, 509–554.

Putnam, H. 1975. The meaning of "meaning." *Minnesota Studies in the Philosophy of Science* 7, 131–193.

Rosaldo, M. 1980. *Knowledge and passion: Ilongot notions of self and social life.* Cambridge: Cambridge University Press.

Schneider, D. 1984. *A critique of the study of kinship.* Ann Arbor: University of Michigan Press.

Sperber, D., and D. Wilson. 1986. *Relevance: Communication and cognition.* Oxford: Blackwell.

Stotz, K., and P. Griffiths. 2004. Genes: Philosophical analyses put to the test. *History and Philosophy of the Life Sciences* 26, 5–28.

Tomasello, M. 1999. *The cultural origins of human cognition.* Cambridge, MA: Harvard University Press.

Tomasello, M., and H. Rakoczy. 2003. What makes human cognition unique? From individual to shared to collective intentionality. *Mind and Language* 18(2), 121–147.

Wimmer, H., and J. Perner. 1983. Beliefs about beliefs: Representation and constraining function of wrong beliefs in young children's understanding of deception. *Cognition* 13, 103–128.

Yanagisako, S. J., and J. F. Collier. 1987. Toward a unified analysis of gender and kinship. In *Gender and kinship: Essays toward a unified analysis* (eds) J. F. Collier and S. J. Yanagisako, 14–50. Stanford, CA: Stanford University Press.

◇

2

Why Religion Is Nothing Special but Is Central

It is proposed that explaining religion in evolutionary terms is a misleading enterprise because religion is an indissoluble part of a unique aspect of human social organization. Theoretical and empirical research should focus on what differentiates human sociality from that of other primates, that is, the fact that members of society often act toward each other in terms of essentialized roles and groups. These have a phenomenological existence that is not based on everyday empirical monitoring but on imagined statuses and communities, such as clans or nations. The neurological basis for this type of social, which includes religion, will therefore depend on the development of imagination. It is suggested that such a development of imagination occurred at about the time of the Upper Palaeolithic "revolution."

Introduction

This chapter reconsiders how we should approach the study of the evolution of religion. The discussion leads me, however, to a more general consideration of the way social cognition has been approached in recent literature. This reconsideration bears in mind the kind of problems that Colin Renfrew has called the "sapient paradox" (Renfrew 1996). The chapter proposes a cognitively and neurologically more probable scenario for the development of religion than certain recent theories that are questioned by the problems he highlights.

The problems I am referring to are particularly thrown into focus by a series of theories that originate in Sperber's suggestion that religious-like beliefs are to be accounted for by a subtle mix of intuitive human capacities based on evolved neurological modules, and certain, very limited, representations that, because they go against the core knowledge that the modules suggest, are therefore "counterintuitive" and "intriguing" (Sperber 1985). The motivation for these theories is to seek an answer to a question. How could a sensible animal like modern *Homo sapiens,* equipped by natural selection with efficient core knowledge (or modular predispositions), that is, knowledge well suited for dealing with the world as it is, hold such ridiculous ideas as: there are ghosts that go through walls; there exist omniscients; and there are deceased people active after death? The authors who hold such a theory of religion give the following answers to this question. First, our core knowledge ensures that, however bizarre such ideas might seem at first, when they are more closely examined, they, in fact, turn out to be mainly disappointingly intuitive. Second, even though beliefs in supernatural things nevertheless do involve a few counterintuitive aspects, if only by definition, these are possible owing to accidental misapplications of core knowledge to domains for which it is not designed. These limited misapplications are, however, so alluring that they make these minimally counterintuitive beliefs spread like wildfire. They thus become key elements in religions (e.g., Boyer 1994, 2001; Pyysiainen 2001).

The problems with these theories that I shall discuss here do not necessarily imply outright rejection. They are what might be called "upstream" objections since they occur even before we consider the main proposals. The first objection echoes a similar one long ago made by Durkheim, but it has been reformulated more recently by Barrett (2004) when he points out that it is odd to account for such a central phenomenon in the history of mankind as religion in terms of minor cognitive malfunctions. My second objection is that those who propose such theories forget the fact that, despite countless attempts, anthropologists have found it impossible to isolate or define a distinct crosscultural phenomenon that, for the purposes of analysis, can be usefully and convincingly labeled "religion."[1] The third problem with such theories is that they explain religion as a product of core knowledge or modular capacities, such as naïve physics, naïve number cognition, naïve biology, and naïve psychology, all of which, with the possible exception of the last, we share with all our anthropoid relatives. Such a proposal is therefore unconvincing simply because no other animal than humans manifests any behavior that is remotely like what is usually called religion. This lack also seems to be the case for all hominids or hominims, apart from post-Upper Palaeolithic modern *Homo sapiens*. In other words, the explanations that I am challenging try to account for a highly specific and general characteristic of modern humans, what they call religion, by recourse to general factors that existed for millions of years before the Upper Palaeolithic revolution when the phenomenon first manifested itself.

The alternative story I propose here avoids these problems. It argues that religious-like phenomena in general are an inseparable part of a key adaptation unique to modern humans. This is the capacity to imagine other worlds, an adaptation that I shall argue is the very foundation of the sociality of modern human society. This neurological adaptation occurred most probably fully developed only around the time of the Upper Palaeolithic revolution.

The Transactional and the Transcendental

For heuristic reasons, a consideration of chimpanzee society can serve as a starting point. I turn toward our nearest surviving relatives in order to stress, as is so often the case in the evolutionary literature, a major difference between them and us. Of course, we cannot assume that contemporary chimpanzee social organization is necessarily like that of early *Homo sapiens*. There is no way to know; especially since the social organizations of the two extant species of chimpanzees are radically different though both are equally closely, or equally remotely, related to us. In this case, it is not the similarity but the difference that is revealing and this difference provides us with something like a thought experiment that enables us to reflect on certain characteristics of human society.

Chimpanzees do not have anything that remotely resembles the many and varied phenomena that have been labeled religion in anthropology. Indeed, this was probably also true of early *Homo sapiens*. But, more importantly, there is also something else that chimpanzees, and probably early *Homo sapiens*, do not have. This is social roles or social groups, understood in one particular sense of the word social.

Of course, chimpanzee social organization is highly complex. For example, the dominant animal is not necessarily the biggest or the one who can hit the hardest. Dominance seems to be achieved as much by Machiavellian politicking as it is by biting. Also, chimpanzees do create long-lasting coalitions, often of females, and these may well dominate the social organization of the group (de Waal 2000). Such roles and groupings are of a type that I call here the *transactional* social. This is because such roles and groups are the product of a process of continual manipulation, assertions, and defeats. This type of social is also found in modern humans.

However, what chimps do not have is the kind of phenomenon that used to be referred to as "social structure" in the heyday of British social anthropology (Radcliffe-Brown 1952). This I shall label here as the *transcendental* social. The transcendental social consists of essentialized roles and groups.

Essentialized roles exist separately from the individual who holds them. Rights and duties apply to the role and not to the individual. Thus, a person who is a professor should act "as a professor" irrespective of the kind of person he/she is at any particular stage in the transactional social game. Similarly, in central Madagascar, as a younger brother, I should walk behind my older brother; as a woman, I should not raise my voice in a mixed gathering. All this applies, however powerful I have actually become, even if my prestige is greater than that of my older brother or of a man.

Essentialized groups exist in the sense that a descent group or a nation exists. These groups have phenomenal existence not because the members of the descent group or the nation are doing certain kinds of thing together at particular moments, or because they have been together doing certain kind of things at particular moments in the sufficiently recent past so that it is reasonable to assume that they retain the capacity to behave now in similar ways. One can be a member of an essentialized transcendental group, or a nation, even though one never comes in contact with the other members of the descent group or the nation. One can accept that others are members of such groups irrespective of the kind of relationship one has had with them or that one can suppose one is likely to have with them. Such groups are, to use Benedict Anderson's phrase, "imagined communities" (Andersen 1983).

As noted above, in stressing the system of essentialized roles and groups, I am emphasizing what British social anthropologists, such as Radcliffe-Brown, were referring to when they spoke of social structure. However, my position is theoretically very different from theirs. For them, the human social was equated with the network of such roles and groups. For me, these phenomena are only a *part* of the social: they are the transcendental social.

The transcendental social is not all there is to human sociality. There is plenty of transactional social in human sociality that occurs side by side or in combination with the transcendental social. The transactional social exists irrespective of the role-like essentialized statuses and the essentialized groups of the transcendental social, though it may use the existence of the transcendental social as one of the many counters used in the transactional game. Human sociality is thus, as Durkheim stressed, double. It has its transactional elements *and* transcendental elements. Chimpanzee sociality, by contrast, is single because the transcendental social does not exist among the chimpanzees.

The double character of the human social can be illustrated by the example of a Malagasy village elder I have known for a long time. By now, he is old, physically weak, and a little bit senile. He has difficulty in recognizing people. He spends most of his days in a foetal position wrapped up in a blanket. Yet he is treated with continual deference, consideration, respect, and even fear. Whenever there is a ritual to be performed, he has to be put in charge so that he can bless the participants. Others behave to him, and he accordingly behaves toward others, as a transcendental elder whenever he is treated with great respect. This does not mean, however, that he is not also within the transactional social system. While as a transcendental elder he is little different from what he was when he was in his prime several years ago, as a transactional player he has lost out completely in the

Machiavellian game of influence, and nobody takes much note of him anymore or of his opinions since in the continual power play of daily life he has become insignificant.

This kind of duality is impossible in chimpanzee society. There, once you are weak or have lost out in the continual wheeling and dealings of power, you lose previous status. In an instant, a dominant animal is replaced in his role (de Waal 2000). A chimpanzee's rank depends entirely on what those it interacts with believe it can do next. Chimpanzees do pay respect to each other in all sorts of ways ... for instance, bowing to a dominant animal, but once this animal has lost out in the power game, this behavior stops instantly. A social position in chimpanzee society never transcends the predictable achievements of the individual. This absence of transcendental roles is where the fundamental difference between chimpanzee and human sociability lies. The Malagasy in the village where this elder lives bow to him just as much now that he is weak as they ever did, even though he has become obviously without transactional influence. It is important to remember, however, that the respect shown to him does not mean that he is an elder all the time. The people who interact with him, and probably he himself, represent him in two ways. These two ways are not experienced as contradictory, but they are clearly distinguished and made visible by the behavior of all concerned. Everybody knows that he is a weak old man whose hands shake and whose memory is going, and people sometimes behave toward him in terms of that representation, even with occasional cruelty. They also behave toward him in terms of the respect as described above. Thus, he belongs to two networks and, although the two are different, the transcendental network is taken into account in the transactional network while the transactional network affects the transcendental network only indirectly; for example, when another person is ultimately able to replace an elder in his transcendental role through revolutionary manipulation (for example, in a traditional African society, convincing people that he is a witch; Middleton 1960).

In order fully to understand the role of an elder such as the one I have in mind, it is essential also to remember that, as a transcendental being, he is part of something that appears as a system, even though this systematicity may be something of an illusion. The transcendental elder implies the existence of transcendental juniors, of transcendental affines, transcendental grandchildren, and so on. The transcendental network involves gender roles, thereby creating transcendental women and men. It is a system of interrelated roles and it is this complexity of interrelations at the transcendental level that most critically distinguishes the human social from the sociality of other species.

This transcendental network also includes what the structural functionalists called "corporate groups," but which I have referred to above as essentialized groups. These are transcendental groups. By this, I mean that, for example, members of a clan are dual. At the transactional level, they differ from each other just as much or as little as they do from people of the next clan. But, in the transcendental social mode, all members of such a group are identical as transcendental members. They are, as is often said, "one body." As one body, they differ absolutely, and all in the same way, from those others in the other clan. The transcendental character of such groups is made all the more evident when we realize that the composition of such groups, whether they are clans or nations, may equally include the living and the dead. Thus, when in the transcendental one-body mode, members can make such bizarre statements as "*We* came to this country two hundred years ago." The transcendental can thus negate the empirically based transactional in which people do not live for 200 years. Similarly, the transactional social can ignore the present physical state of an elder as easily as it can ignore death and individuality. The transcendental network can with no problem include the dead, ancestors, and gods as well as living role holders and members of essentialized groups. Ancestors and gods are compatible with living elders or members of nations because all are equally mysterious and invisible, in other words transcendental.

The Transcendental Social and Religion

This indissoluble unity between the living and the dead and between what is often called the "religious" and the "social" has never been better explained than by Igor Kopytoff "Ancestors as elders in Africa" (Kopytoff 1971). Although the article is phrased as a criticism of earlier work by Fortes, it actually follows the latter author closely. Kopytoff points out how in many African languages the same word is used for living elders and for dead ancestors whom, it has often been said in the literature, Africans "worship." This is because in a sense, in the transcendental sense, they are the same kind of beings. Kopytoff stresses how both ancestors and elders have much the same powers of blessing and cursing. This leads him to assert that to talk of "ancestor worship," and thereby to suggest something analogous to an Abrahamic notion of a distinction between material and spiritual beings, is an ethnocentric representation that imposes *our* categorical opposition between the natural and the supernatural, or between the "real" and the religious, onto people for whom the contrast does not exist.

I accept much of Kopytoff's and Fortes's argument and want to expand it. What matters here is that if they are right, there is no reason why we cannot reverse the argument, something that Kopytoff himself suggests. If dead ancestors in an "ancestor-worshipping society" are the same ontological phenomena as elders, then elders have the same ontological status as ancestors. If there is a type of phenomenon that merits the appellation ancestor worship, which suggests the kind of things that have often been called religion, then there is also elder worship or elder religion. And since elders are part of a system, there is, in the traditional sense, junior religion, descent group religion, man religion, woman religion, and so on.

Although to talk in this way may be fun, we have to use our words with the meanings that they have historically acquired. So it might be better to rephrase the point and say that the phenomena that we have ethnocentrically called religion and the phenomena I have referred to as the transcendental social are part and parcel of a single unity. This implies that the English word *religion*, inevitably carrying with it the history of Christianity, is misleading for understanding such phenomena as ancestor worship since, in such cases, there is not the same boundary between the "supernatural" and the "natural" as that perceived to occur in societies caught in the history of the Abrahamic religions. A boundary nonetheless exists also in these cases, and it occurs between two types of social: the transcendental social including the phenomena that have been called religion and the transactional social. This boundary is clear in the kind of society I am referring to and explains the two different ways of acting toward the Malagasy elder noted above.

The inseparability of the transcendental social and the religious is not only manifested in cases of so-called ancestor worship. Hinduism is a phenomenon that is often assumed to be comparable with the Abrahamic religions, but such an equation is misleading for the same reasons as apply to the African examples discussed previously. For example, Fuller begins his study of popular Hinduism by pointing out that a wife should, and indeed does, at some moments, treat her husband in the same way as she treats the gods. The same gestures and bodily positions are used in both cases in performing *puja* and the husband can thus be said to be a "god" to his wife in the Hindu sense of god. The point is that here also the transcendental social husband and wife roles are part of one single overarching transcendental hierarchical social system that includes the gods (Fuller 1992).

The societies I have discussed above clearly present a challenge for the kind of theories referred to at the beginning of this chapter, that is, the theories advocated by, among others, Boyer. This is because they explain a phenomenon that can only be distinguished from a greater whole—the transcendental social—by using a contrast between the religious and the secular that is borrowed from a relatively modern system of representations that simply does not apply in their cases. Consequently, I shall argue that it is the greater whole in its totality, that is, the transcendental, that needs to be explained. However, such a redefinition of the project presents an obvious difficulty. If Boyer is wrong to take a specific type of society, those with religion, to represent the human condition in general, is it not equally wrong to take specific other societies, those discussed in this chapter so far, as representing human nature?

Historical Excursions

In what follows I argue that this is not so because societies with religion are the subsequent product of an inessential and superficial modification of the societies discussed above.

A full demonstration of this point would require much more space than is available in this short chapter. What follows is therefore nothing more than a tentative sketch of what such a proposal would look like. In order to explain how a certain state of affairs occurred for some, and only some, human groups, I move to a historical argument. I argue that it is in certain specific historical circumstances (admittedly of great importance for the majority of mankind though not for all) that the kind of phenomena we call religious take on a separate appearance that seems to distinguish them from the more inclusive transcendental social.

The creation of an apparently separate religion is closely tied to the history of the state. It has long been noted that the "religious" and the "political" were inseparable in many early states such as Mesopotamia, Egypt, China, and the Early Andean states. Frankfort long ago argued that in ancient Egypt the pharaoh was a visible god interacting on a compatible footing with the invisible gods. The organization of the state was part of the divine order (Frankfort 1948). The ancient Egyptian kingdom was part of an explicit cosmic ordering of space and time. The recurrence of the flooding of the Nile was represented as the consequence of the repetitive cyclic action of the gods, including the pharaoh. The world was centered on the capital with distant uncivilized, barely human, peripheral peoples far from its center. Egypt was, to borrow the Chinese phrase, the empire of the center. All this is the familiar attribute of what has been called divine kingship, whether it is that of the Swazi kingdom, the Indic states, or the Mesopotamian city-states.

The transcendental representation of such states was not all there was to political organization. There were also other available transactional representations of the state, pharaoh, time, and space. In much the same way as the Malagasy elder is dual, it was also possible to see the pharaoh in more straightforward terms, and that was in spite of the prodigious efforts that were made to transform him through his palace and his tomb into an empirical manifestation of his transcendental side.

The transcendental construction of such states is also accompanied by another corollary process. The development of the Merina state in Madagascar in the eighteenth and nineteenth centuries shows how the construction of the symbolic state is accompanied by a partial destruction and *reformulation* of the symbolism of its subjects. Thus, certain key attributes of elders/ancestors were forcibly transferred from local descent groups to the king and his palace (Bloch 1986). Interestingly, a similar process involving the diminution of the transcendental social of subjects for the benefit and construction of the royal transcendental has been examined for early Egypt by Wengrow (2006).

Thus, the royal centralized transcendental construction depends on the partial destruction or at least transformation of the symbolical system of subjects. In Madagascar, the focus of the symbolism of the subjects migrated, thanks to violent state encouragement, from the house to the tomb, as the palace became the symbolical house of the kingdom with the ruler as its central "post" (in Malagasy, *Andry*, which is also the root of *Andriana*, the term for "ruler" or "lord"; Bloch 1995). Similarly, and in more detail, I described how circumcision, a descent group ritual, became orchestrated by the state and how certain aspects were taken away from the elders to become constitutive elements of grand-state occasions. The descent groups *lost* key elements to the representative of the state and were punished if they attempted to perform the full ritual independently (Bloch 1986).

Since the transcendental social and the religious are identical in such systems, it is not just the religious that is reorganized in a centralized state; to a certain extent, it is the whole transcendental social that is sucked into a centralized, organized, organic-seeming system. The creation of this transcendental holistic image of the complete kingdom, including gods and men, thus requires the creation of the incompleteness and disorganization of the subjects' transcendental social, which can only be made complete in the kingdom.

Subsequent to the symbolic centralization of the state, another rather different process occurs. States are unstable, and political systems continually collapse. That causes a new problem. When the royal state collapses at the hand of its enemies, the subjects find themselves bereft because the construction of the state had previously made them transcendentally incomplete and the state, after its collapse, is no longer there to complete them.

The same Malagasy example can again illustrate this point. The growth of the Merina kingdom in the nineteenth century had led to the circumcision ritual being partly taken out of the transcendental construction of descent groups and being placed in the realm of the symbolical construction of the kingdom. However, in 1868, when the Merina kingdom became disorganized, in part owing to the influence of Christianity, the ruler failed to perform the royal circumcision ritual. At that point, a popular movement arose which sought to *force* him to perform it.

Why did the subjects feel bereft by the royal nonperformance when originally the ritual had been their privilege? Why should they seek the state that in many ways exploited them? Because, given the previous process, when the state collapsed, they were left with nothing but their incomplete transcendental social and, for reasons that I cannot explain, it seems as if the deprivation process is irreversible. Thus, when the state, having confiscated a large part of the transcendental social so as to create its own ordered pseudototality of cosmic order, then collapsed, a totalizing transcendental representation without its political foundation remained, floating in mid air, so to speak. This begins to look like what we call religion. For example, the collapse of the political base of the transcendental social may lead to the occurrence of these ritual, sacred, pseudoroyal systems of Africa that so fascinated Frazer, where as Evans-Pritchard said, the king "reigns but does not rule" (Evans-Pritchard 1948). It is what leads to shadow "states" that only exist in mystical form as spirits that possess mediums. Examples of these are found among the Shona or in western Madagascar where they were caused, Feeley-Harnik argues, by the collapse of the political as a consequence of colonial rule (Feeley-Harnik 1991). This is also what explains the bizarre institutions of contemporary European monarchies. These post-state states are "religions," that is, phenomena apparently distinct from the rest of the transcendental social.

The Abrahamic religions offer another example of the process. The historian of Judaism and of early Christianity, J. Z. Smith, argues that Jewish monotheism must be understood as the product of a longing for the unified, centralized, holistic transcendental Mesopotamian city-states with ziggurats at their center. These were a kind of state that the Jews, as minor peripherals to that system, hardly ever managed to achieve for themselves, or, when they did, did so on a tiny fragile scale. Early Judaism is therefore also a transcendental incomplete residue: religion. This residue was modeled on the Mesopotamian prototype with, at its center, the ziggurat in a purely religious form, that is, the temple in Jerusalem (Smith 1982).

With this sort of situation, we therefore get religions that are only apparently separate from the transcendental social state, but this separation is always uncomfortable and unfinished and it leads to the kind of flirting processes between state and religion that has characterized history in much of the Abrahamic world. At least in Europe and those great sways of Asia and Africa that are still under the ghostly spell of ancient Mesopotamia and Egypt this flirting takes various forms. One form of the process involves new states taking on, ready made, one of these politically detached religions issued from clearly different political entities. Rome was an example of the process. Imperial Rome became one of these centralized systems where political conquest led to the creation of a transcendental social representation of the state through making incomplete the transcendental social of subjects. Yet the transcendental construction never worked very well and when Rome got into even more trouble than usual, the system broke down. This led to the adoption of foreign and abandoned center religions "hungry" for the recovery of their lost politico/transcendental social element, for example, Judaism, other eastern religions, and ultimately, one of the many forms of Christianity. Rome was therefore taking on the religious side of a centralized system from a collapsed tiny city-state as a late attempt at reorganization of a unified transcendental (Beard et al. 1998).

The process repeated itself. When, in the seventh century, the Franks began to develop centralized entities in western Europe, they picked up Christianity and, so to speak, "put it on" with modifications to make it fit. One of the most spectacular moments was when Charlemagne in 800 invented a ritual that made him the Holy Roman Emperor with bits borrowed from the Old Testament, from Frankish rituals, and of course, above all, from Roman rituals (Nelson 1987). The other form of the relation between religion and the state, made necessary by their previous separation as a result of the collapse of a centralized unit, is for the religious bit to try to grow back its lost political undercarriage. Again and again, the popes attempted this. The Ayatollah Khomeini was more successful. Most of the movements that have been called millenarians try this sort of thing. Mormon history furnishes a particularly interesting example. Joseph Smith started the Mormon religion in the eastern USA for people who were heirs to a Christian religion that at many removes was heir to a long history of trouble between the religious-like pretensions of the state and the state-like pretensions of religion. However, the Mormons were in a place where the state was weak and, unusually, where the totalizing cosmological pretensions of post-state religion were strikingly incoherent, largely because they were meant to apply to a country not included in the cosmology of the Bible. So the Mormons put that to right by finding a Gospel that did mention the New World and its inhabitants and, in their creative enthusiasm, began to rebuild the political part of the destroyed transcendental entity. Not surprisingly, this annoyed the other state in Washington and they had to try to build it up in the desert, which, amazingly, they just about succeeded in doing. At the center of this renewed unitary entity, where the transcendental social and religious were again to be an inseparable totality as in ancient Egypt or Mesopotamia, they built their temple: a temple that looks strikingly like a ziggurat.

Conclusion

The point of these historical excursions is to suggest that the separation of religion from the transcendental social in general is, even in the places where it appears at first to exist, superficial and transient. In any case, this superficial phenomenon has occurred in human history only relatively recently.

It is this transcendental social in its totality that should be our focus. It is what distinguishes the human social from that of other closely related animals, such as chimpanzees. It is a unique characteristic and an essential part of human sociality, which, as often suggested, is *the* fundamental difference between humans and other anthropoids. An explanation of its occurrence cannot thus be in terms of a minor evolutionary adaptation, or misadaptation, as is suggested by Boyer-type theories.

Such a conclusion is negative, but it is possible to propose a more positive and fruitful one.

What the transcendental social requires is the ability to live very largely in imagination. We often act toward elders, kings, mothers, and so on, not in terms of how they appear to the senses at any particular moment but as if they were something else: essential transcendental beings. Once we realize this omnipresence of the imaginary in the everyday, nothing special is left to explain concerning religion. What needs to be explained is the much more general question, how it is that we can act so much of the time toward visible people in terms of their invisible halo. The tool for this fundamental operation is the capacity for imagination. It is while searching for neurological evidence for the development of this capacity and of its social implications that we, in passing, will account for religious-like phenomena. Trying to understand how imagination can account for the transcendental social, and incidentally religion, is a quite different enterprise to accounting for the religious in terms of modules, or core knowledge, which, in any case, we share with other primates. Unlike core knowledge, imagination does seem to distinguish us from chimpanzees and perhaps also distinguished post-Upper Palaeolithic humans from their forebears.

A number of recent writers have suggested something along the same lines. In a book by Paul Harris about imagination, the author shows how the ability to engage spontaneously in pretend play begins very young and develops in a multitude of ways such as creating "imaginary friends" and other forms of explicit make-believe. Such imagination practice seems essential for normal human development. Nothing like that occurs in other species. Clearly, this capacity is necessary for engaging in the transcendental social as defined above, inevitably including the religious-like. The selective advantage this form of sociality procures explains its evolutionary potential. It is central to human life. Harris suggests this centrality in an adventurous introduction when he notes that the first evidence for such a capacity is the cave paintings of Europe dating back to ca. 40,000 years ago (Harris 2000). He might have gone a bit further back to what has been called the Upper Palaeolithic revolution, one feature of which was the first suggestion of transcendental roles found in grand burial.

Again, in a parallel argument, also taking empirical data on ontological development as its starting point, Hannes Rakoczy connects the imagination and the transcendental social even more explicitly (Rakoczy 2007). In his work, and that of his co-workers, this is referred to as "status functions" though it is as yet little developed. However, the argument is strikingly similar to and totally congruent with that proposed above. Like Harris, Rakoczy and his co-workers do not explicitly address the topic of religion, but according to my argument religion is automatically subsumed under this type of discussion of the social. To explain religion is therefore a fundamentally misguided enterprise. It is rather like trying to explain the function of headlights while ignoring what motorcars are like and for. What needs to be explained is the nature of human sociability, and then religion simply appears as an aspect of this that cannot stand alone. Unfortunately, the recent general discussion on social cognition does not succeed in doing the job that is needed to understand the transcendental social either. This is because, for the most part, it has considered the human social as an elaboration and an expansion of the type of social found in other animals, especially other primates (Dunbar 2004). This is useful but it obscures a fundamental difference between humans and others. Such an approach only pays attention to the transactional, or the "Machiavellian" social, since that is what is shared by, for example, baboons and humans. It ignores the uniquely human transcendental social that represents a qualitative *difference* with other nonhuman socialities. What is essential to understand is the evolution of this specificity. Concentrating on that equally unique human capacity—imagination—seems the most fruitful approach in that enterprise and, in passing, we will also account for religion since it is nothing special.

Note

1. Boyer insists that he is not talking about religion in the usual sense, but he does not define what he is talking about and he has no problem in entitling his books *The naturalness of religious ideas:*

a cognitive theory of religion and *Religion explained: the evolutionary origins of religious thought.*

References

Andersen, B. 1983. *Imagined communities: Reflections on the origin and the spread of nationalism.* London: Verso.

Barrett, J. 2004. *Why would anyone believe in god?* Walnut Creek, CA: Alta Mira Press.

Beard, M., J. North, and J. Price. 1998. *Religions of Rome,* vol. 2. Cambridge: Cambridge University Press.

Bloch, M. 1986. *From blessing to violence: History and ideology in the circumcision ritual of the Merina of Madagascar.* Cambridge: Cambridge University Press.

———. 1995. The symbolism of tombs and houses in Austronesian societies with reference to two Malagasy cases. *Austronesian Studies* August 1995, 1–26. (Taipei.)

Boyer, P. 1994. *The naturalness of religious ideas: A cognitive theory of religion.* Berkeley: University of California Press.

———. 2001. *Religion explained: The evolutionary origins of religious thought.* New York: Basic Books.

de Waal, F. 2000. *Chimpanzee politics: Power and sex among apes.* Baltimore, MD: Johns Hopkins University Press.

Dunbar, R. 2004. *The human story.* London: Faber and Faber.

Evans-Pritchard, E. E. 1948. *The divine kingship of the Shilluk of the Nilotic Sudan.* Cambridge: Cambridge University Press.

Feeley-Harnik, G. 1991. *The green estate: Restoring independence in Madagascar.* Washington, DC: Smithsonian Institution Press.

Fuller, C. 1992. *The camphor flame: Popular Hinduism and society in India.* Princeton, NJ: Princeton University Press.

Frankfort, H. 1948. *Kingship and the gods.* Chicago: Chicago University Press.

Harris, P. 2000. *The work of the imagination: Understanding children's worlds.* Oxford: Blackwell.

Kopytoff, I. 1971. Ancestors as elders in Africa. *Africa* 41, 129–142.

Middleton, J. 1960. *Lugbara religion.* London: Oxford University Press.

Nelson, J. 1987. The Lord's anointed or the people's choice: Carolingian royal rituals. In *Rituals of royalty* (eds) D. Cannadine and S. Price, 137–180. Cambridge: Cambridge University Press.

Pyysiainen, I. 2001. *How religion works.* Leiden, The Netherlands: Brill.

Radcliffe-Brown, A. R. 1952. *Structure and function in primitive society.* London: Cohen and West.

Rakoczy, H. 2007. Play, games and the development of collective intentionality. In *Conventionality in cognitive development: How children acquire representations in language thought and action* (eds) C. Kalish and M. Sabbagh), 53–67. *New directions in child and adolescent development*, no. 115. San Francisco: Jossey-Bass.

Renfrew, C. 1996. The sapient behaviour paradox: How to test for potential? In *Modelling the early human mind* (eds) P. Mellars and K. Gibson, 11–15. Cambridge: McDonald Institute.

Smith, J. Z. 1982. *Imagining religion: From Babylon to Jonestown.* Chicago: University of Chicago Press.

Sperber, D. 1985. Anthropology and psychology: Towards an epidemiology of representations. *Man* (N.S.) 20, 73–89.

Wengrow, D. 2006. *The archaeology of early Egypt. Social transformations in north-east Africa, 10,000–2,650 BC.* Cambridge: Cambridge University Press.

◆

3

Truth and Sight

Generalizing without Universalizing

The English word "evidence" is based on the Latin verb *videre*: to see. Familiar phrases such as "seeing is believing" or the assurance that something must be true because "I saw it with my own eyes" are everywhere. Such observations and many others all bear witness to a well-established European connection between seeing and truth which, as the *Shorter Oxford Dictionary* tells us, is so often associated with evidence.

Such a link seems very ancient. Thus Thucydides says that, in contrast to that based on hearsay, the only true history is that based on the authority of sight (*autopsia*): "of the two ways of knowing, through the eye and the ear, only the former gives us a true picture," because accounts based on memory distort and lie.[1] Saint Paul, for his part, in a famous Platonic mood, makes the same equation when he tells us of the dark glass which, by interfering with our sight, keeps us from the full truth. The idea that seeing is a guarantee of truth continues in less ancient times. Thus, the greater truthfulness of what is *seen* over what is reported through language is a major theme in the writings of Augustine (Stock 1996), and Bacon, Hume, Condillac (Roos 1999), and the empiricist/sensationalist philosophers generally all make the point. This type of argument is found, with modifications, in Kant. In a completely different way, writers such as Broca, after having noted the prominence of the lower brain in nonhuman primates, especially the olfactory bulb, see evolution as the progress of the development of "higher" senses, above all sight, over "lower" senses, especially smell (Dias 2004).

But what do such recurrences of an association between truth and sight mean for the anthropologist? Are they more than a manifestation of a particular turn of our own culture, which, once again, we might naïvely take to be universal? Such a classic form of professional scepticism does not, at first, seem to be borne out by a cursory inspection of the ethnographic record. In an article to which I return below, Stephen Tyler (1984) informs us that the association of truth and sight recurs in all Indo-European languages, including Hittite, and also in many other language families. Ranging even more widely, the comparative linguist Viberg (2001) sees the association as extremely common in all languages. Certainly, a random trawl through ethnographic sources comes up with many examples from all over the world. Thus Strathern (1975) and Robbins (2001) tell us that the New Guinea Islanders they studied are obsessed with the unreliability of language and, by contrast, stress the truth of knowledge obtained through sight. Taylor confirms that the Amazonian Achuars are similar.[2] Izard also tells me that much the same is true of the Mossi of Burkina Faso.[3] According to Christopher Pinney (2008), Indian nationalists, the British colonial administration, and the old lady in the film convinced that photographs show gods who are real, are all influenced in their attitude to photography by the belief that what the lens sees is so.

There are some dissenting voices, however, that give examples where sight is not linked to the notion of truth. A number of anthropologists report ethnographic cases which purport to show that, among this or that group, another sense, usually hearing, is valued above vision (Feld 1982; Gell 1995; Tyler 1984).[4] The question of the relative significance of the different senses has also come up in the scholarly tradition. Some, especially those eighteenth-century philosophers who engaged with Molineux's problem (would a man, blind from birth, who was then cured recognize through sight those objects which he had only felt before his cure?), most notably Diderot in the *Lettre sur les aveugles,* tangled endlessly with the question of the relation and hier-archy of touch and sight.

The presence of possible exceptions, based on a few exotic ethnographies, which are then used as negative evidence against an assumed universality, is a familiar form of argu-ment in anthropology. Such rhetoric was the cause of the popularity of work such as that of Margaret Mead. Indeed, it might seem that the only defence against such negative argument is either to challenge the reliability of the supposed exception, as was famously done by Derek Freeman (1983), or to broaden and weaken the claim to universality. Thus, we might modify the proposition that sight is always associated with truth to one that merely claims an association between truth and knowledge through the senses in general. However, even such a less specific claim would also be vulnerable in a different and more fundamental sense, in much the way that all generalizations in kinship theory have been attacked (Bloch and Sperber 2002; Needham 1971) by pointing out the obvious fact that the details of every ethnographic case are different. Lumping these cases together would thus be a case of begging the question, an example of mere reduction-ism, where it seems that a universal category is created when in fact the cases only have in common what the definition created by the observer has arbitrarily decided is significant.

These are familiar ways in which generalizing claims in anthropology have been attacked, and they are not without basis. Such destructive tactics have been effective to such an extent that many in the discipline have abandoned all attempts at grand theory and shudder at any claims that any-thing nonparticularistic could exist in cultural phenomena. However, the problem with such timid nihilism is that the prominence of recurrences in the ethnographic record, such as the association of truth and sight, can only be ignored through acts of blatant theoretical bad faith. But, given the soundness of the objections, we are left with the question of what we are to do about them.

In this short chapter I propose to give an example of pre-cisely how we might attempt to generalize about a phenom-enon such as the nonuniversal but frequent recurrence of the association between truth and sight without ignoring the important antiuniversalist points referred to above. In doing this, I hope to give one example of how anthropology, in the original sense of the term, is still a possible enterprise, in spite of the criticisms such an approach has had to face in the last thirty years. But, before engaging in grand theorizing, I invite the reader to take a detour via an ethnographic case.

Zafimaniry Theory

During a recent period of research in the remote Zafimaniry village in Madagascar where I have been working for so long, I tried out a new research strategy, new for a social anthropologist at least, in order to understand what might be called "Zafimaniry ethno-psychology." This consisted in demonstrating in front of my fellow villagers a well-known psychological experiment concerned with the cognitive development of children. This was in order to hear how the adults interpreted what they saw their children doing, as they observed the tasks they were asked to do. In other words, I put ordinary people, who had never heard the word "psychology" and who, for the most part, could neither read nor write, in the position in which professional psychologists normally place themselves.

The experiment referred to is called the "false belief task." It has been considered in cognitive psychology as being of great significance since it seems to reveal a critical moment in the child's cognitive development. The false belief task, in the version I used, consists in asking a child where a person who saw an object placed under one hat will look for it when they return after a spell outside the house, during which period the subject has seen the object being switched to another hiding place by the experimenter. Adults and older children normally say that the person will look for the object under the hat where the person saw it placed before he or she left the house, but where they themselves know it no longer is. This is taken to mean that they understand that the person who left the house holds a false belief. Young children, by contrast, say that the person returning will look for the object at the place where it actually is. In most of the psychological literature at least, this is usually taken to mean that the young child has not yet understood that other people act in terms of how they *believe* the world to be; a notion that is obviously necessary for someone to realize that others could hold false beliefs about the world. Such a difference between the older children who rightly predict that the person will look where they *believe* the object is and the younger ones who predict the person will look for the object where it actually *is* is striking and thought provoking. It raises much broader questions, concerned not only with child development, but also with what our understanding of others and their minds requires in order to act competently in the social world.

It is precisely because this experiment raises such fundamental questions and because reflecting on its significance leads to such fundamental reflection about the human mind and the nature of human sociability that it seemed interesting to see how the Malagasy villagers would rise to the challenge. I thus used the Zafimaniry witnesses of the experiment and their surprise at the difference between the responses of the younger and older children to trigger wide-ranging discussions on, among other things, the nature of thought and language, child development, and the cognitive differences between humans and other animals. These discussions took the form of animated conversations in which all sorts of ideas were aired. Certain of the musings of the villagers were expressed with a good deal of hesitation and others were much contested. Some propositions, however, came loud and clear and were acknowledged as obviously right by everybody present. It is only these that I consider here.

Among these broadly agreed propositions was the idea that thought is, at bottom, a matter of organizing action so that it achieves desired ends. In the villagers' view two things follow from this pragmatic way of understanding mind. First, nonhuman animals are as capable of thought as humans, since pigs, for example, will think of turning up during the preparation of food in order to eat what peelings might be available, and since fleas will think of hiding in the seams of clothing in order not to be caught. Secondly, and this follows inevitably from the previous point, the villagers were quite clear that thought is independent of language, since they well know that animals strategize their actions but do not talk.[5]

However, my informants did not undervalue language for all that. They were adamant that language was a key factor in the superiority of humans over animals. Their affirmation in this matter led me to ask them what language was for, if it was not, as they asserted, necessary for thought. The answer that was invariably given is that language enables humans to lie. According to Zafimaniry theory, speech, and lying, which speech renders possible, is an extra technique, not available to animals but available to humans, that enables older children and adults to obtain by means of deceit what they have desired in their thoughts. Furthermore, and in response to the experiment, the villagers also argued that this refined technology for Machiavellian gratification, not possible for animals, is also not available to very young humans, since infants obviously do not know how to speak. Language is something that develops as human children mature and learn. Such reasoning was the basis of the villagers' interpretation of the false belief task in terms of lying. It explains why young children, like animals, cannot lie because they do not yet have language, or, at least, sufficient control over language. Infants fail the false belief task because they have not yet reached the developmental stage when they so control language that they are able to lie. This is an ability that requires, in the first place, an understanding that others can hold false beliefs, since otherwise there would not be any point in lying.[6]

The villagers also made clear that such ideas about language, motivation, and thought have important further implications. The first concerns their description of the experience of the social. The second concerns the experiential side of evidence. I take these two in turn.

In the discussions that followed the observation of the false belief task, the social was described as a dangerous and exciting matter. It involves living among chattering individuals who, like you, are seeking to further their own ends by fair means or foul, and who therefore use all the tools available as speaking human adults. This makes normal life risky because it involves being among people endowed with, and indeed continually using, their capacity for lying. At every step, therefore, there is a danger that one acts in terms of a world that is false. This feeling is often expressed in the fear that those who falsely profess to love you might, really, be trying to poison you.

Secondly, since it is assumed that pragmatic deceit is the default form of social life, this makes claiming truthfulness for what one is saying no trivial matter; therefore doing so must be clearly distinguished from the everyday. This leads to a continual emphasis in discourse which makes clear that normal interchange is not strongly claiming that what one is proposing is true, so that, when one will actually want to claim truthfulness for one's declaration, these instances will really stand out from normal dialogue. This attitude has the effect that, for example, when one is asking for information, the most common answer is a semi-indignant *asa*: "search me," followed for greater emphasis by *tsy fantatro*: "I don't know," and then the information requested is offered. Similarly, this information, when it is finally volunteered, is either preceded or followed by the word *angamba*, meaning "perhaps."

All this tentativeness can thus then contrast with those moments when one *does* want to be believed categorically. I may want to say, "There really *is* a mad dog in the village!' To do this one can either follow the assertion by the word *marina*, usually and appropriately translated as: "It's true," or, for even greater claim to truth, say, "Hita maso!," literally, "It was seen by my own eyes!"

The Zafimaniry, and all the Malagasy I know, are thus yet another example of the many people around the world who associate statements claiming the authority of sensations, and especially sight, as being powerful evidence of truthfulness. But their discussions following their observations of the false belief task take us even further. They willingly explained why sight is so important: this is because it is verification that avoids the treacherousness of language used in social life, since social life is a matter of dealing with speaking individuals who can hide the truth in order to further their own ends and trick you. The Zafimaniry thus, continually, implicitly and explicitly, operate a strong contrast between information obtained through ordinary speech, which they rhetorically mark as uncertain, and which they associate with lying, and information obtained through the sense of sight.

But why do they use knowledge through the senses, and sight in particular,[7] to contrast with the treachery of the social? The answer is implicit in all their discussion of language. What they seem to be saying is that, via language, truth is vitiated by Machiavellian social intentionality. Sight, on the other hand, as it is thought about in Zafimaniry theory—if one can call ideas that are usually only implicit "theory"—

does not involve the dangerous imagined intentionality projected by the source of knowledge. What one sees has no intention to represent itself, falsely or otherwise; one may mistake what one sees but that's your fault, not, as in the case of linguistic dialogue, the result of the intention of the schemers with whom one is in a relationship.

Machiavellian Intelligence

The question that the above suggests, however, is the following. Even if my interpretation of what the Zafimaniry told me in response to their witnessing the false belief task is accurate, why should that tell us anything about human beings in general, the definitional aim of anthropological theory? Is the above simply one more local theory, to be added to the stamp collection of local representations that anthropology sometime seems to see as its only purpose?

As a first step in arguing against such a typically frequent pessimistic conclusion, we should, first of all, remind ourselves of the problem of recurrence that such insistence on the uniqueness of each case creates for a culturalist approach. If we take the particularistic stance, this becomes incomprehensible. Indeed, the similarity of discourses in the different ethnographic cases to which I refer is even greater than suggested at first. It is not only that we find, again and again, an association between sight and truth, we also find this associated with the distrust of what one might call "hearsay evidence," for the reason that this may be vitiated by the treacherous intentionality that characterizes ordinary social life. In other words lying is linked, as it is so clearly for the Zafimaniry, to what the philosophers call theory of mind, the continual reading of intentionality that human communication uniquely implies and that ultimately makes deceit easily possible. Furthermore, this potential treacherousness is most often seen as the product of the capacity for language that makes lying possible.

Thus, we cannot ignore the fact that so many people, in different cultures all around the world, are saying similar things again and again. Such recurrences are a challenge that anthropology should not dodge by finding occasional counterexamples. Then, there is another type of recurrence. What ordinary people argue, according to ethnographic reports, such as the one I briefly supplied above for the Zafimaniry, is interestingly very close to a set of very differently styled propositions that are not the product of ethnographic inter-pretation but are typical of the theories of some evolutionary scientists reflecting on human sociability and language.

Evolutionary theory has again and again stressed the problem caused by the potential that theory of mind, hu-man intentionality, and human language create by making deceit so easy. There is no place here to discuss this massive literature that stresses the point that the supremely well-adapted tool for human sociability—language—creates at the same time and by its very nature, a major problem for individual members of a community in that it places them at risk of being misled. Scholars of many different kinds see the awareness and significance of this fact as central. This fundamental point is found in the work of many anthropolo-gists (e.g., Bateson 1951; Cosmides and Tooby 1992; Knight 1998; Rappaport 1979; Sperber 2001), leading biologists and theoreticians of evolution (e.g., Dawkins and Krebs 1978; Krebs and Dawkins 1984; Maynard Smith and Harper 1995; Waddington 1960), and linguists (Dessalles 2000; Lyons 1977), to name only a few. The views expressed are varied, but, like the Zafimaniry, all these writers are agreed that the complexity created by our ability to read others' minds—that which makes language use possible (Sperber and Wilson 1995)—exposes older children and adult members of the species to a risk that exists only to a limited extent for other animals, if at all: that of being misled by conspecifics and thereby acting against one's own interest.

We might conclude from this massive scholarly endorse-ment of Zafimaniry theory that, in this matter, there is little to be said other than that the villagers are right. But, if this is so, it raises a fascinating question. How can this agreement have come about given the totally different circumstances and contexts in which scholars and, in the case of the Zafi-maniry, unschooled shifting cultivators live?

The answer must be that there is something in the hu-man condition that is accessible to the understanding of different members of the human species irrespective of history, living in however different circumstances around the globe, that produces cognate representations. In this

case, it means that the experience and the awareness of
the experience of social life and its dangers, of human intentionality and of the reading of human intentionality, are,
in their most fundamental aspects, universal. To assume
this implies that the representations people have are *about*
this something—the dangers of living among communicative intentional beings—and that this same thing exists
independently of the representations people have of it. And,
indeed, it is extraordinarily difficult to imagine a human
group unconcerned with deceit and lying. Of course, this
does not mean that the representations of the dangers of
language, deceit, and lying are determined by what they
are about. It would be as wrong to forget the specificities of
each case as to forget the recurrences. Inevitably cultural,
historical, and personal circumstances will lead to variation
in styles, directions, and contents. How far purely intellectual speculation on this matter is pushed also varies.
For example, scientists are professionally trained to push
their reflection, and some groups of people, among whom
I would include the Zafimaniry, seem to have developed a
greater aesthetic orientation toward theoretical speculation
than others. There is room for much variation. It is possible that the kind of speculation I have been talking about
is totally absent in some cases. This, however, would not
invalidate the argument I am developing, simply because
these exceptions would not remove the existence of frequent
recurrences. In spite of variation, all this theorizing, when it
occurs, is about the universal awareness of the same thing.
And this awareness is sufficiently constraining to the images
that can be produced to cope with it that frequent similarities in representations will occur. This is what explains the
recurrences. But because the process of representation is
also affected by other important factors—cultural, historical, and so on—we will *only* have family likenesses among
the representations of this same awareness.

The commonality of these representations has a further
cultural implication that, this time, has a practical side to it.
The awareness of the potential treacherousness of the social
and of the tool that language offers for deceit is recognized
in all the ethnographic cases cited not just as a subject of
speculation but also as a major political problem and a threat
to in-group sociability. As a result, various practices and
institutions are developed explicitly in order to cope with this

threat, of which legal devices, such as those discussed by Anthony Good (2008), are the most obvious example. And, in parallel, the specificity of the threat of deceit that exists in language leads to the development and the valuing of devices and ideas for guaranteeing truthful knowledge that is not caught in the web of human intentionality and speech.

This is the explanation for the recurrence that this essay seeks to explain: the association of truth and the senses and, more particularly, sight. With the type of psychology that the awareness of deceit creates, the idea that what is seen is more truthful than what is reported in speech seems an obvious way to go in order to bypass human intentionality and deceit. Again we have a weak form of determinism. The total causal path is the following. The reality of the human social and the potential of human language lead necessarily to an awareness of the dangers of deceit and lying. This universal awareness strongly influences the representations we find of the social, of language and of deceit, hence the recurrences. These types of representations regularly, but not necessarily always, predispose to the association linking truth and sight. It is thus not surprising that this particular path is so often chosen, though, of course, there might well be cases where it is refused.

And we can go even further in the line of weak determinism that has guided me throughout this essay. Another case of recurrence that the ethnographic record throws up can be seen to have the same root. This is the similarity displayed by techniques of divination found in so many places around the world. These techniques commonly aim to produce truthful propositions that, unlike other forms of telling, do not involve language and its inevitable corollary, human intentionality. The famous techniques of Azande divination are of this type, as are such practices as tea leaf reading, astrology, and many others. The point about all these is that they use devices that produce truthful answers that are the fruit of a form of causation, such as physiological configuration, in the case of the reading of entrails, or physics, in the case of throwing stones in the air, that is not social. (This, of course, creates the well-known problem that the answers must then be interpreted and translated by humans who reintroduce intentionality and hence fallibility.) Such divination techniques seem to tell the truth through what can be *seen* in states of affairs not brought about by the intentionality of human minds, and thus implicitly recognize the dangers of the social and of human language with its potential for lies.

This seems to be, in part, what Martin Holbraad (2008) argues for Cuban divination, which, like Azande divination, is also taken by its practitioners as truth-telling by definition. According to Holbraad, divination is ontologically creative, a process that seems somewhat mysterious if ontology is taken to mean an exhaustive account of the world as it is. If that is so, it is difficult to understand how it could be added to. However, the sheer demonstration of an effect that seems to be the product of naïve laws of physics yet that, as we know (cf. Spelke et al. 1995), we innately recognize as necessarily true, seems a more convincing explanation of the feeling of ontological certainty that Holbraad is describing. The revelation of divination would thus seem to be, for the practitioners, a peep at the world as it appears to the senses, in contrast to the treacherous representations peddled by others.

Interestingly the truth-telling powers of divination seem to have a similar basis to the naïve attitudes to photography discussed by Pinney, where, at first, all sorts of people were convinced that cameras told the truth because they were machines: in other words, because human intentionality was not involved in their powers of representation.

Here again the line of causation, from the shadowy awareness of the nature of the social and of the implications of the human mind to actual practices, seems a tempting and, therefore, frequently followed path. But, for all that, it is neither a necessary nor a rigidly mapped-out path. Thus, if divination techniques are commonly similar, they are also each and every one different, and there may well be societies where such techniques are totally absent. This variation and occasional absence, however, would not contradict the kind of argument I have been developing here. As so many anthropologists rightly, if somewhat trivially, insist, the social world we live in is the product of dialogue, of discourse, of culture, and so on. But this does not mean that these dialogues, discourses, and cultures are not *about* something that people, thankfully to a certain extent, apprehend, and this something, as the psychologist James Gibson stressed, itself suggests nonrandom affordances that are, again and again, represented (Gibson 1977).

But there is more to this question than simply the constraints that come from what the representations concern. The ability to read each other's minds and the dangers this creates is a fundamental matter for the adaptation of *Homo sapiens*. This ability necessarily evokes the ideas about the dangers about deceit that concern my Malagasy informants and evolutionary psychologists. However, unlike theory of mind itself, which can operate below the level of consciousness, and usually does, knowledge about deceit and lying needs to be, and evidently is, available to consciousness, if only so that it can be guarded against. This is clearly of crucial importance for all who live in a human-type society, and therefore it is quite likely that, as the evolutionary psychologists argue, we are probably innately predisposed to detect cheaters. But even if this is so, such ability cannot be just automatic since it requires consequent conscious protective actions that, I would argue, are likely to be organized in dedicated institutions. These include, among others, the ones mentioned above: certain divination techniques and legal systems.

This long and tentative line of causation is the story that can explain the familiar mix of recurrences and variations that I have been concerned with throughout this essay. The universal consciousness of the presence of lying and deceit in society logically implies the possibility that people can hold false beliefs. This awareness can be, and often is, used as a handle for creating, in varying degrees of elaboration, a representation of the mechanisms of the nature of mind, a representation that is constrained both by what mind is like and by our social need to be on guard against lying. Peeping at the mind by using the handle of mistaken knowledge is what the inventors of the false belief task intended to do, and it is also what the Zafimaniry and the people from the other ethnographic cases evoked seem to be doing when, for example, in observing the experiment, and also in many other moments of their lives, they try to explain the difference between the younger and the older children. Knowledge of lying and deceit is thus *only* a handle, hence the relative variation, but it is a good handle that we may be predisposed to use, hence the recurrences and the profundity of the reflection.

And this sort of weak determination works the other way, too. The consciousness of the problem of deceit, so often carrying with it an associated and overdetermined theory of mind, leads to recurrences in institutional means to enforce the truth and also to imaginative speculation about what might establish truth. These speculations, in turn, lead to recurrent rhetorical formulations such as: "It's true, I saw it with my own eyes!," or in Malagasy, considerably more elegantly, "Hita maso!"

Notes

Although this is a short chapter, it has often involved me in reaching out beyond my usual competence. As a result I have had to rely on the help of many fellow scholars. I wish to acknowledge the following for their generous help either in reading an earlier draft or suggesting relevant leads to the literature: Rita Astuti, Nelia Dias, Matthew Engelke, Michel Izard, Eva Keller, Gerard Lenclud, Gloria Orrigi, Nathaniel Roberts, and Åakon Viberg.

1. I am grateful to Gerard Lenclud for drawing my attention to this quotation.
2. Pers. comm., 2005.
3. Pers. comm., 2005.
4. I have to admit a certain scepticism as to how far the particular claims of Gell and Feld are based on a general ranking of hearing over sight within these cultures and not simply on certain contextually specific evaluations: for example, hunting in dense forests or the typical New Guinea association of unseen birds with ancestors. In any case, it is not clear how far these authors intend to push their argument. Such hesitation, on the other hand, does not apply to the most categorical of the anthropologists. Stephen Tyler, in an article already referred to, and which ironically supplies us with a great number of examples of the coupling of truth and sight, nevertheless concludes that "the hegemony of the visual is not universal" and that empiricism as a folk theory is a peculiarity of certain grammars. The counter-example he gives to set against the mass of the *visualists,* whom he dismisses, are the speakers of Dravidian languages. His evidence is based on a form of primitive Whorfian examination of Dravidian verbs for knowing, which are taken to offer an easy window to thought. But even if we accept his epistemology, there are serious reasons to doubt what he says about this particular example. Thus, in a personal communication, Nathaniel Roberts tells me that in Tamil, the most spoken Dravidian language, the word most used for "to know" is *theriyum* (root form: *theri*), for which the standard modern Tamil dictionary in the first place defines: "(1) be visible; be seen; (2) (of eyes) see; to perform the function of seeing."

5. This work is ongoing, but for a somewhat fuller discussion of this material, see Chapter 7.
6. This point requires further elaboration not possible here.
7. It is probably because language is associated with hearing that sight is usually favored over hearing, the only other serious contender among the senses as the source of complex wide-ranging information.

References

Bateson, G. 1951. Conventions of communication: Where validity depends upon belief. In *Communication: The social matrix of psychiatry* (eds) J. Ruesch and G. Bateson, 212–227. New York: Norton.

Bloch, M., and D. Sperber. 2002. Kinship and evolved psychological dispositions: The mother's brother controversy reconsidered. *Current Anthropology* 43, 723–748.

Cosmides, L., and J. Tooby. 1992. Cognitive adaptation for social exchange. In *The adapted mind: Evolutionary psychology and the generation of culture* (eds) J. H. Barkow, L. Cosmides, and J. Tooby, 163–228. New York: Oxford University Press.

Dawkins, R., and J. R. Krebs. 1978. Animal signals: Information or manipulation? In *Behavioral ecology: An evolutionary approach* (eds) J. R. Krebs and N. B. Davies, 282–309. Oxford: Blackwell.

Dessalles, J.-L. 2000. *Aux origines du langage: Une histoire naturelle de la parole*. Paris: Hermes.

Dias, N. 2004. *La mesure des sens: Les anthropologies et le corps humain au XIXème siècle*. Paris: Aubier.

Feld, S. 1982. *Sound and sentiment: Birds, weeping and song in Kaluli expression*. Philadelphia: University of Pennsylvania Press.

Freeman, D. 1983. *Margaret Mead and Samoa: The making and unmaking of an anthropological myth*. Cambridge, MA: Harvard University Press.

Gell, A. 1995. The language of the forest: Landscape and phonological iconism in Umeda. In *The anthropology of landscape: Perspectives on place and space* (eds) E. Hirsch and M. O'Hanlon, 232–254. Oxford: Clarendon Press.

Gibson, J. J. 1977. The theory of affordances. In *Perceiving, acting, and knowing: Toward an ecological psychology* (eds) R. Shaw and J. Bransford, 67–82. Hillsdale, NJ: Lawrence Erlbaum.

Good, A. 2008. Cultural evidence in courts of law. *Journal of the Royal Anthropological Institute* 14 (s1) S47–S60.

Holbraad, M. 2008. Definitive evidence, from Cuban gods. *Journal of the Royal Anthropological Institute* 14 (s1) S93–S109.

Knight, C. 1998. Ritual/speech coevolution: A solution to the problem of deception. In *Approaches to the evolution of language* (eds) J. Hurford, M. Studdert-Kennedy, and C. Knight, 68–91. Cambridge: Cambridge University Press.

Krebs, J. R., and R. Dawkins. 1984. Animal signals: Mind reading and manipulation. In *Behavioral ecology: an evolutionary approach* (eds) J. R. Krebs and N. B. Davies, 380–405. (Second edition.) Oxford: Blackwell.

Lyons, J. 1977. *Semantics*, vol. 2. Cambridge: University Press.

Maynard Smith, J., and D. G. C. Harper. 1995. Animal signals: Models and terminology. *Journal of Theoretical Biology* 177, 305–311.

Needham, R. 1971. Remarks on the analysis of kinship and marriage. In *Rethinking kinship and marriage* (ed) R. Needham, 1–34. London: Tavistock.

Pinney, C. 2008. The prosthetic eye: Photography as cure and poison. *Journal of the Royal Anthropological Institute* 14 (s1) S33–S46.

Rappaport, R. A. 1979. *Ecology, meaning, and religion.* Berkeley: North Atlantic Books.

Robbins, J. 2001. God is nothing but talk: Modernity, language, and prayer in a Papua New Guinea Society. *American Anthropologist* 103, 901–912.

Roos, S. 1999. Consciousness and the linguistic in Condillac. *MLN* 114, 667–690.

Spelke, E., A. Phillips, and A. L. Woodward. 1995. Infants' knowledge of object motion and human action. In *Causal cognition: A multidisciplinary debate* (eds) D. Sperber and A. J. Premack, 44–78. London: Oxford University Press.

Sperber, D. 2001. An evolutionary perspective on testimony and argumentation. *Philosophical Topics* 29, 401–413.

Sperber, D., and D. Wilson. 1995. *Relevance: Communication and cognition.* Oxford: Blackwell.

Stock, B. 1996. *Augustine the reader.* Cambridge, MA: Harvard University Press.

Strathern, A. 1975. Veiled speech in Mount Hagen. In *Political language and oratory in traditional societies* (ed) M. Bloch, 185–203. London: Academic Press.

Tyler, S. A. 1984. The vision quest in the West, or what the mind's eye sees. *Journal of Anthropological Research* 40, 23–40.

Viberg, Å. 2001. The verbs of perception. In *Language typology and language universals: An international handbook* (eds) M. Haspelmath, E. König, W. Oesterreicher, and W. Raible, 123–163. Berlin: De Gruyter.

Waddington, C. 1960. *The ethical animal.* London: Allen & Unwin.

◊

4

Teknonymy and the Evocation of the "Social" among the Zafimaniry of Madagascar

Introduction

Names are words, and as words they are constituent elements in speech acts. Alone, or in combination with other linguistic phenomena, they are sounds that, as a result of the conventions learned by speakers of a particular community, evoke mental responses in the minds of hearers or speakers (see Lambek 2006 for a very similar theoretical position).

It is important to begin a discussion of names in this rather pedantic way because too often in the literature names are considered in terms of the old and dangerous semiotic model of signifiers signifying signifieds. As has been argued by vom Bruck (2001), words, including names, pace Lévi-Strauss (1962, Chapter 6), are not classifiers and to see them as such is misleading. First, such an approach gives far too fixed an image of meaning, forgetting that the usage of names cannot be separated from pragmatics and that names are used to "do" an almost unlimited number of things. Names, therefore, are tools used in social interaction, which can be put to ever-new uses. Second, the use of names is a constituent part of the social interactions in which they are used. Such uses are never isolated acts, but are parts of acts. Third, names, whether used in reference or in address, are only one among many ways of referring to people. They do not form a bounded system, but must be considered with other designating devices that include, inter alia, eye contacts, pronouns, titles, gestures, and kinship terms. This means that the choice involved in using names must always be understood in terms of the available alternatives.

Thus, in this chapter, I will not limit my attention to the analysis of *names*, strictly speaking. I also have to consider many other types of words that would normally be called *titles, kin terms,* and so forth. I will be concerned with placing all these words in the world of interactions.

But there is an even more important reason why the semiotic model is misleading. It implies that words ultimately reflect the world, and that this is what they signify. If this world includes the social world, as it does in much anthropological writing, it is given a referential quality of realism that is quite false. Words such as names do not signify the social; rather, they are one of the ways in which phantasmogorical images are given fleeting phenemonological existence. As we shall see in the example to be discussed here, different types of names may suggest a number of such images that may be quite contradictory. One image may be of an ordered encompassing moral whole that I call the "transcendental social." Images of this kind are accorded particular authority by important people, but this is all the more reason for not allowing ourselves to be tricked into according them a false realism. On the contrary, it is a reason for examining the ways in which such imagery is given its apparent concreteness.

The Zafimaniry

This chapter concerns a relatively small group of people, approximately 30,000, who call themselves the Zafimaniry. They live in the eastern forest of Madagascar and are, by the standards of that country, and for a number of historical reasons, surprisingly culturally homogeneous (Coulaud 1973; Bloch 1992).

Much of Zafimaniry rhetoric concerning the process of life and death is similar to what has been described for many groups in the highlands of Madagascar in that it is governed

by the general principle involving a movement from the fluidity, wetness, and lack of social role of infancy and childhood
to the strong individual vitality of early adulthood that is
in turn replaced by the growing stabilization of the person,
both geographically and socially, with age. This "placing" is
accompanied by the fading of individuality of all kinds, including sexual and gender identity. This process ends when
the mortal body is replaced by or merged into an enduring
artifact, usually a tomb. For highland Malagasy people such
as the Merina, the focus on tombs is part of the creation of
an image of an ordered "social" system that in no way reflects practical life (Bloch 1971). In the Zafimaniry case, by
contrast, the house takes on the role of the tomb. This shift
is theoretically treacherous because the noncorrespondence
between the image of a "society" of houses and practical life is
far less obvious than the contrast between a society of dead
people in tombs and the everyday doings of the living. As a
result, we must exercise even more care in the analysis of
the Zafimaniry data if we are not to be misled into merging
the two levels.

The Zafimaniry house is, above all, an inseparable part
of the evocation of a successful marriage; a marriage that
produces and sustains progeny who, in their turn, continue
the process. The ordered image that I call the "transcendental
social" is made of these marriages/houses.

Such a house is established when a man brings a wife
and usually their children to the structure he has begun to
build. In settling in a permanent manner, they can start to be
considered part of an encompassing moral order. This material form of the union is seen as particularly manifested in
the conjunction of the central post of the house, associated
with the man, and the furnished hearth, associated with the
woman. At first, the house is an impermanent structure, but
with time it becomes more permanent, as hardwood replaces
perishable materials. It also becomes more beautiful as carvings increasingly decorate the wood.

The centrality of the conceptual inseparability of the
fruitful human union with the house as a building and its
location can be seen particularly clearly when we consider
the nature of what might be called the Zafimaniry concept
of adultery. This adultery occurs when a man or a woman
(usually a man) brings another person *into* the house and has

sexual intercourse there. This is a very serious fault that, if discovered, usually leads to the breakdown of the marriage and social opprobrium. By contrast, extramarital sexual liaisons that take place *outside* the house are considered, at least by those not directly involved, as minor and amusing peccadilloes.

The evoked growth of the house/marriage does not end with the death of the original couple because the children, grandchildren, and great-grandchildren are expected to continue to strengthen the building (and therefore the original couple), decorate it with carvings, and gather there to ask for blessings from the original pair. At this stage, however, it is no longer living people who are beseeched, but the house itself that has become the enduring material existence of the original couple after death in the continually constructed image of the "social." Furthermore, a successful house/marriage may become the center of a village as the descendants build their own houses around the ancestral sacred house, the house of the founding marriage. Thus the transformation of the bodies of the married pair into a localized thing, their house, and finally into an inhabited and settled place is achieved and becomes the governing principle of the Zafimaniry "transcendental social" (Bloch 1995).

Names

The word normally translated as *name* in standard Malagasy is *anarana*; its meaning corresponds fairly well to that of the English term. The Zafimaniry usage is very similar. *Anarana* can be used somewhat neutrally to refer to the words that designate places and towns. Applied to people, it has a wide semantic field similar to that of the English term *name* in that it can be used not only to designate individuals or groups but also to refer to their "reputation" or even their rank. Indeed, as we shall see, *anarana* is never hierarchically neutral when applied to people. *Anarana* can also be used in less familiar ways, most importantly in prayers addressed to the ancestors when the term *anaran'dray*, *lit*: "the name of the father" evokes the ancestors on the father's side, and the term *anaran'dreny* evokes those on the mother's side.

Personal Names

Children are given names that I call "personal names" because they are linked to individuals and to individuals only, and do not link the child to anybody else, as, for example, surnames do in the West. Personal names do not, therefore, evoke a "social" system in any way; only the "individual." The "individual" is an equally immaterial entity whose phenomenological existence is created by acts such as using personal names.

These personal names are used in both reference and address. Personal names are given eight days after birth in the case of a girl and seven days after birth in the case of a boy. The difference is explained by the fact that seven is a "strong" number that girls "could not bear." The ritual of name giving is simple, usually involving little more than a dozen people. The purpose of the ritual is said to make the child become *mazava,* which is a word best translated as "clear," but which has many other associations such as making truthful or ancestral (Bloch 1995). In the case of the naming ritual, the word *mazava* is used, according to my own gloss and to the rather more hesitant gloss offered by my informants, to convey the idea of the "definite" character of the child's entry into a clear world out of the hazy darkness of the womb.

The main act of the ritual consists in winding the child's umbilical cord around a dried bamboo, which is then lit and burned so that it and the cord are consumed. This act is said to "illuminate" the child. The idea that "clarity" comes from burning this type of dried bamboo is a recurrent and important Zafimaniry symbolical theme that occurs in a number of other contexts, and it is indeed true that the white flame of this particular dried bamboo illuminates with striking brightness.

The burning of the bamboo and the cord is accompanied by a rather simple incantation asking for blessing, which is addressed to nobody in particular. The invocation is repeated six times, an auspicious number used in all Zafimaniry blessings. The actual words used mean "blessed be the name."

This first personal name given to a child involves a choice followed by a consultation with a diviner astrologer who may approve it, warn against it, or suggest an alternative name on his own initiative if some kind of danger is anticipated. In the latter instance, the diviner is understood to select a more auspicious name according to the obscure principles of his art. This type of name given by a diviner is intended, above all, to draw attention away from the child and to mislead those vague forces of evil who might want to harm it. As a result, the name is often disparaging and hides the pleasure of the parents in the birth. Such names are called "bad names" because their negative character protects the child by warding off evil forces (Njara 1994). Indeed, the use of any name for a child draws attention to its birth and thus always carries a certain danger, probably from the malice of those who might be jealous of the parents' good fortune. For this reason, as elsewhere in Madagascar, the personal names of young babies are commonly avoided in public by the parents and close kin, and instead replaced by an unflattering generic term such as "little rat." Consequently, only a very few people know the name of a child until it is quite old. The evoking of the unique person is thus delayed.

If the name is chosen by the family, there is no absolute rule about who decides. It might be the parents, but most commonly it is one of the maternal grandparents, especially the maternal grandmother, who makes the choice because Zafimaniry women usually go back to their parents' house for the birth of the child, and it is there that the naming ceremony takes place, usually under the maternal grandmother's supervision and authority. It is also possible for almost anyone to ask that the parents give a child his or her name as a favor, and such a request is very difficult to refuse. It usually involves the name giver making a present to the parents, a chicken for example. Such a procedure does not, however, necessarily imply a continuing relationship between the name giver and the child, which would be part of some "social" order.

If we except the so-called "bad names," the names of young children seem to be chosen on a wide variety of not very serious ad hoc principles. Personal names may allude to the names of people of significance including, but not exclusively, kin. They may allude to places, events, or things, or a combination of these different factors but not in any systematic way. Many names refer to the previous history of the mother or of other people. Thus, a girl in one of the villages

I studied is called *Soafamahamaizina,* which means "sweet but which then renders dark." The "bad" part of this name is sometimes said to refer to the fact that she had a twin who died at the time of her birth and (it was explained to me) the evil of this death, which still vaguely clings to the survivor by association, is prevented from harming her because it is openly acknowledged through the use of the name. Allusions in a name can take the form of incorporating the whole of an alluded name or one segment of it. As a result, given names may form a phrase whose meaning can be deciphered and is often ironic. However, it is also often the case that such names involve no recognizable word or phrase.

All these principles can be mixed in the most fanciful and playful of ways. In the same village, I knew a child called *Zafimiaraka,* which means "the grandchild who is together." However, I was told that the real reason for his name was that his father had been given the baptismal name Jean-Paul, which in his case and quite unusually, was regularly used to refer to him, probably because of his enthusiasm for the church. Jean-Paul, to Malagasy ears, sounds like *Za,* or perhaps *Zafy.* The word would then mean "together with his father Jean-Paul" and this was cited as the (improbable) reason for his name. I don't know whether this story is a joke (it probably is because the most obvious meaning of the name is the first one), but it is a joke that had been so often repeated that its playful character had faded and, by the time I heard it, was believed to be the true motivation for the name, by some people at least.

Personal names do not necessarily indicate the gender of the child. Some names are associated with girls and others with boys, but many are neither. Personal names really only reflect the impulse of the moment when they were given and a concern with the child's gender might not have been upper-most at the time. The optional reference to gender yet again reflects the nonsystematic character of Zafimaniry naming.

This bewildering freedom of choice, in which naming is not governed by hard and fast principles and is often enough based on a whim or a pun, shows that a newborn child is not yet an entity with a fixed place in an organized world. Rather than a successor to previous generations, he or she is evoked as a kind of social monad and a subject of speculation. The child is a phenomenon that has appeared in the clear light of the burning bamboo, but remains fundamentally alone, outside any encompassing system. This non-"social" character of the child's name accords well with the often-repeated phrase that children, especially boys, are "animals." This qualification is not without an element of admiration because it implies strength and liberty, but above all, it stresses how the child has not yet been bound and domesticated by parenthood, morality, and the social. This does not mean that the child is of little or no value; on the contrary, the individual existence that the personal name evokes for a child is envied by older Zafimaniry who are about to be sucked up into gradual impersonality by their imaginative incorporation into the encompassing system that teknonyms evoke.[1]

Teknonyms

The period of childhood, when the personal name is appropriate, is theoretically brought to an end by marriage. Marriage in the Zafimaniry sense, however, is not a change brought about in a moment, but is a process drawn out over many years. It requires the building of a house, and its defining feature is parenthood. One cannot be truly married until one has had at the very least one child. The establishment of a house and parenthood are both necessary, but it is the parental element that is directly reflected in the uses of names.[2]

The rule is apparently simple. Once a person has borne a child, they should never again be addressed, nor referred to politely, by their personal name. They must be addressed by a teknonym. The teknonym is based on the name of the first child born to the parent, whether this child survives or not and irrespective of its gender. The principle underlying this rule is categorical: Parenthood marks the entry into Zafimaniry "society," not birth. To address a person who has borne a child by their personal name is to treat them like a child/animal and to refuse to represent them as having taken the first step to becoming part of a larger established order consisting of fruitful marriages, houses, and localities. Name use is a not insignificant part of an order created and continually re-created through the evocations of communication and intercourse. In this sense, one can say that it is the birth of the child that makes the parent a member of "society."[3]

However, if the teknonym marks the beginning of the creation of the social person and the imagination of "society," it inevitably has a contradictory correlate: the beginning of the disappearance from the phenomenology of experience of the individual monad that is evident in the way children are named. Thus, although the teknonym honors, it also depersonalizes. It replaces the individual by his or her role. This is a process that is not necessarily positive and is often resisted in minor but not insignificant ways (Bloch 1999). The depersonalization caused by the use of teknonyms is somewhat similar to the effect noted by the Geertzes for commoner Balinese (Geertz and Geertz 1964). They argue that Balinese teknonyms lead to genealogical amnesia and the effacement of ancestral identities. Such processes are less obvious among the Zafimaniry because elaborate genealogies are in any case rare in highland Madagascar. But what Zafimaniry teknonyms create is perhaps a premature manifestation of a similar process, an effacement of the living as they go through their lives.

Another aspect of teknonyms is that they are the only terminological link between spouses because father and mother are both referred to by similar teknonyms because they always involve the name of the same child. By contrast, the earlier stages of the marriage process are not reflected in naming practices. This reflects the fact that the marriage hardly gains social significance until it has reached the stage of child production. To put the matter differently: It is not possible to be a socially recognized *couple* without being a socially recognized father or mother. In contrast to what is the case in many other parts of Madagascar, single mothers are not normally addressed by a teknonym so are not "social" mothers.[4] To address or refer to a single mother by a teknonym implicitly evokes the shadowy putative existence of a father for the child, who would be addressed by the corresponding teknonym if only he could be located. Much the same pattern applies to fathers, although single fathers are recognized only in quite exceptional circumstances.

Practice in the use of teknonyms is much less clear-cut than the simple principle outlined previously, however.

Although one should be called after one's first child, in fact dead children are often forgotten and imperceptibly replaced by living ones, especially those who are present and successful in the village. This also has the unintentional and uninstitutionalized effect that because women tend to marry out of the village, boys' personal names are more often used than girls' personal names as the basis of teknonyms.

Other factors that are linked to particular circumstances and show the suppleness of the system can also influence which child is chosen for his parents' teknonyms. They include the personal affection of a parent for a particular son or daughter, or the interest the person addressing the parent has in evoking a particular child. Aspects of the triangular relationship between the parents, the child, and the person addressing the parent can also have an effect. For example, if I am particularly familiar with a child called Koto, and if I want to stress our relationship when speaking to his parents, I will address them as "mother of Koto" or "father of Koto," even though Koto is not their first child and in spite of the fact that they are normally addressed by a teknonym based on their first child's name.

Such contextual practice shows how the use of teknonyms is not simply a matter of identifying a person by a conventional sign; a teknonym also contains a proposition. These propositions can be paraphrased, for example, as "You are the mother of Koto, and I am showing you respect because you are the parent of such a powerful person," or "You are the father of Koto, and because of my link to him I want to link myself to you." Like all propositions, such propositions are always expressed and understood as having a communicative purpose that explains their place within the context of a speech act. This purpose, as always, depends on the relationship between, and the attitudes of, speakers and intended hearers.

Teknonyms and the Status of Elder

Teknonyms are, first of all, the recognition and assertion that the person addressed or referred to is a mother or father. Thus, the mother of Solo is *renin'Solo* because *reny* means mother, and his father is *rain'Solo* because *ray* means father. But to understand fully the frequency of use of the teknonyms, another aspect needs to be taken into account.

Because of the existence of Solo, both his father and mother are also something else, something we can gloss as "parents" where the term *parent* is a translation of the Malagasy *raiamandreny*. This is a word used in most of Madagascar and among the Zafimaniry. The word *raiamandreny* is a unit and not a phrase, but it is composed of the word for father *ray*, the word for mother *reny*, and an emphatic word for "and": *aman*. Thus it can be said literally to mean "father as well as mother." Now, for the Malagasy, as is the case for the English word *parent*, a person becomes, by definition, a *raiamandreny* by the simple fact of having had a child, and inevitably this is implied and proposed by the use of a teknonym.

However, the term *raiamandreny* also has other connotations, which explain why it is usually translated as "elder" in the literature on Madagascar, probably by analogy with African elders. Indeed, in a phrase such as "the *raiamandreny* of the village," the term is used in ways very similar to the way terms for "elder" would be used on the African continent. Nonetheless, the fact that the Zafimaniry term does not refer to age but rather consists of the phrase "father and mother" is highly significant for understanding Zafimaniry concepts of seniority. Obviously, it highlights the crucial social significance of parenthood, but this is common to teknonyms in general. What is particularly significant is that being called a *raiamandreny* also depersonalizes, but in a more fundamental way than from the use of a teknonym. This depersonalization becomes particularly clear when people become important supports and leaders of the community (i.e., *raiamandreny* in all senses of the term). Respected *raiamandreny* are people who ideally do not speak or act for themselves because they embody the community as a whole, present, past, and future. They are thus the channels through which the ancestors make their presence felt as being together with the living. When acting out this role, *raiamandreny* dress unobtrusively and speak very quietly, almost inaudibly, with their heads bowed. It is as if they should disappear as people and appear as nothing other than a small constitutive part of the "social." Such *raiamandreny* have already become almost nothing *but* parents or ancestors (the latter are by definition parents), and soon they will die and nothing of the individual will remain. Or instead they will survive in a transformed sexless, bodiless, unindividuated state in the combined form of their house and their progeny. For the "social" exists, not only in the give and take of human intercourse but also in shared interpretations concerning houses and villages, those human artifacts that leave no place for individual human beings. Significantly, it is rare to use *any* name to address people who have reached the stage of full *raiamandreny*-hood and procreative success in life. To do so would imply an intrusion, as if using a name constituted an attempt to evoke their particular identity and to deny the depersonalized, corporate entity they claim and appear to be.

This respectful depersonalization, which is often manifested in the avoidance of any name for address, and even of any indicative form of address such as the use of kinship terms, pointing, or even second-person pronouns, explains a particularly surprising Zafimaniry practice: referring to people simply by the name of their village. Such a usage is particularly respectful because it seems to treat people as if they were always representatives of their locality or as part of a place. And, of course, in a sense this is precisely what Zafimaniry ideology suggests. People become houses through fruitful marriages through fruitful houses; and fruitful houses and fruitful marriages in turn become villages. Or, to put it another way, villages are fruitful marriages, and their inhabitants are products of these fruitful marriages.

All this has implications for the uses of teknonyms. Young people, who have borne a child, but whose house is not yet completed and whose own parents are still alive, could be referred to as a *raiamandreny* because they have become parents ipso facto. But to do so in any normal context would be bizarre and cause a good deal of mirth because young people are not elders; that is the basis of an established and growing family. They therefore are still individualized as the mother or father of so-and-so, and have not yet become a fruitful conjunction of male and female located in a house that will continue after their deaths.

The avoidance of calling young parents *raiamandreny* has additional effects, even coloring the use of teknonyms. Although it would be most offensive to call or refer to someone who has just borne a first child by their personal name because this would deny the recognition due to them, it would, nonetheless, be odd to refer to them by a teknonym because this would imply aspects of parenthood, notably the status of elderhood, that they have not yet achieved. As a result of this ambiguity, young parents are often referred to by no name at all, or, if need be, indicated merely by a pronoun, usually by the more "familiar" forms of the pronouns or by a kinship term.

Young Zafimaniry parents are therefore in something of a name no-man's-land because they are parents but not yet truly elders. All local terms combine the two statuses as if they were one. However, with more children and grandchildren, the teknonym normally becomes established for reference and because the only alternative (to use a personal name) would amount to denying the person the legitimate place in the moral order of society that their hardening house and reproductive success demonstrates. In address, however, the name is little used in casual speech, but when the teknonym is used in this way, it marks the speech act as being of importance and involving the rights and duties of the addressee, rights and duties that they are in the process of acquiring as a result of the "social" corporate being they are realizing in themselves.

Raiamandreny Status and Gender

It is within the framework of this general process of depersonalization, whereby individuals become houses and places, that the issue of gender is best considered.

As noted, personal names often indicate whether the person is female or male, but this is best seen as an aspect of the individuality that the name celebrates. As an individual, a person has many attributes that the personal name comments on, often in a very indirect manner. The gender of a person is quite naturally an important attribute, so it is not surprising that it is often picked up in this way, although always together with other traits. However, as is characteristic of personal names in general, this is not systematic because the personal name does not imply that the individual is part of a system; quite the opposite.

Such a lack of systematicity around personal names contrasts with the uses of teknonyms, which indicate the place of the individual in an evoked "social" system. This place is gendered by the nature of teknonymy that, inter alia, distinguishes mother from father. But noting a gendered element to teknonyms needs further qualification. First of all, I would argue that any gender proposition that the teknonym contains is always less salient than the parental proposition. Second, and equally significant, the gender opposition implied by the father/mother dichotomy gradually becomes subordinated to the nongendered element. This becomes clear when we bear in mind the development implied in the uses of teknonyms noted previously. With time, being a *raiamandreny*, which begins with the mere fact of being a parent, becomes increasingly associated with, and ultimately replaced by, the "elder" aspect of the meaning of the term. This "elder" aspect of the term is not gender-neutral, but it stresses that the Zafimaniry concept of elder/parent *encompasses* fatherhood and motherhood *together*. This, after all, is the literal meaning of the term, and both men and women can be qualified as *raiamandreny*. Becoming an ever more "social" being means that the incomplete character of fatherhood and motherhood is gradually replaced by a complementary and encompassing depersonalized parenthood of fatherhood *and* motherhood. This encompassing combined parenthood becomes the house, a totally impersonal yet beautiful artifact, fixed in a particular place, whose very construction also combines the masculine and the feminine.

Necronyms

In the past, important people were given a new name after their death that was used whenever they were referred to. The main significance of this name was that it made it possible to avoid the names used in life. Nowadays, such names are rarely given because the ceremony during which they used to be inaugurated seldom takes place, at least in Christian villages. This means that necronyms are used only for ancestors from long ago, usually when referring to the founders of famous villages, and even then very sparingly.

However, even today one does not casually refer to the dead by name. An often-quoted phrase is "One does not use names for no reason." To do so shows a lack of respect, but above all it seems to bring the unsettling presence of the dead, as individuals, too close. Among the Zafimaniry, as elsewhere in Madagascar, the ancestors are somewhat ambiguous figures. On the one hand, they are the source of blessing as parents; on the other, they are also suspected of being individuals who, jealous of the living, have resisted depersonalization. After all, as noted previously, the depersonalization process leading to the status of *raiamandreny* is not wholly positive; it implies giving up the self and the pleasures the self enjoys. The dead as ancestors are, therefore, perhaps jealous of the sensuous life of living people, especially young living people. As such, they are possible sources of trouble (Astuti 1994; Graeber 1995; Cole 2001). Referring to the dead as a group by the general term for ancestors, *razana*, or contacting them as houses suggests their more beneficial protective side, but calling them by individual names evokes the particular individual who could be troublesome. Only at rituals asking for blessing do Zafimaniry elders move away from the more depersonalized representations and call the ancestors by name, usually as part of a list. It is as if only in this way can their full power be brought into the arena of the living, but this remains a dangerous business to be undertaken only by respected elders who have taken many precautions. Even then, they address the dead very quietly, so that nobody, except those immediately concerned who stand nearby, can hear the names spoken.

The same discomfort can be seen in the recent practice of writing the names of the dead on monuments near or on burial spots. It has become common to place a wooden cross against the stone covering the tomb; it is on these wooden crosses that are inscribed the name of the deceased and the date of their death. The practice is probably due to the influence of the missionaries. However, the Zafimaniry are careful to make these crosses from wood that rots quickly. The symbolism of the decay of the crosses echoes the non-Christian symbolism of traditional Zafimaniry funerals, in which the wooden pole that was used to carry the corpse to the burial site was left to rot on the spot. Similarly, as was the case for these poles, it is believed that the decay of the timber crosses parallels and is a sign of the decay of the soft parts of the body. This is particularly important because only when these parts have disappeared will it be possible to carry out rituals that involve entry into the tomb. The wooden crosses, however, create a new aspect of significa- tion because it is also the name of the deceased that disap- pears from the location of the tomb. This fits well with the Madagascar-wide gradual depersonalization of the person through life, but also particularly well with the characteristic Zafimaniry de-emphasis of the tomb as an ancestral site and the accompanying emphasis on the house.

The last fifty years have seen one development, however, that works against the disappearance of the names of the dead from everyday consciousness: the fact that rich Zafi- maniry have employed Betsileo stone masons to build either the traditional commemorative stone monuments that stand outside villages or stone tombs of the highland type. On both these types of artifact, Betsileo masons have often inscribed the names of the deceased with the date of death. Such stone tombs represent such a radical departure from Zafimaniry conceptions of what is appropriate after death that people say of those who commission them that they are "becom- ing Betsileo," in this way expressing the idea that they are completely outside the evoked traditional "social" system. Such an action reflects a general rejection of what it means to be a Zafimaniry. The same is not true of the names that the Betsileo masons often carve on the stone monuments. There the inscribed names merely cause discomfort. Indeed, I remember asking a companion about those names while standing right in front of such a monument. After pausing with embarrassment, he assured me that the writing had become obscured by moss and lichen and consequently could not be made out. In fact, I had no difficulty in deciphering it nor, do I believe, did he.

Baptismal Names

Totally unconnected to the traditional naming practices are the names given in Christian baptism. These are always French, although often pronounced in an unrecognizable Malagasy way. The reason for these names is that most Zafi- maniry consider their villages to be Christian—sometimes Catholic and sometimes Protestant. In these Christian villages, many children are baptized and are given what the priest or the pastor believes are suitable Christian names. The villages I know best were officially Catholic, and a French missionary would come once a year or so to baptize children presented by their families. Christian names so obtained were more widely used and better known when I first worked among the Zafimaniry in 1971. By the late 1990s, the influence of the Catholic Church had waned considerably, and fewer children were baptized. Of those who were, their Christian names were almost never used except in the presence of the priest, and most were simply forgotten. Only a few individuals were regularly called by these names as an alternative to what the Zafimaniry call "Malagasy" names.

Certain names given by the priest remained important, even in recent years. Occasionally, Christian names were used because other available names had become forbidden through the dictate of some taboo or other. Usually, however, the use of such a name involved the recognition of the particular individual's strong commitment to the church, and, almost always, also their general orientation toward the outside and toward the urban bureaucratic modern world.

The Jean-Paul referred to previously is one of these persons for whom the baptismal name was normally used. He is an enthusiastic and sincere Catholic, and it was in his house that the priest stayed on his pastoral visits to the village. He had taken full advantage of the possibilities that the church offered, especially in terms of education, and had succeeded in schooling two of his children so well that they had gone on as boarders to a local Catholic school and had ultimately become urban dwellers. One was making a living in business while the other worked in the government administration. It was no doubt his own wish to be addressed as Jean-Paul, and when he was called in this way, the use of the words evoked the world to which he was aspiring and in which he had been successful by Zafimaniry standards. When used by others, the choice of his baptismal name normally marked the respect that his success earned in the village.

However, matters are not so simple and straightforward. It was evident that the name was also used with varying degrees of irony and a rather bitter irony at that. To understand the nature of this irony, one needs to appreciate the ambivalence that is felt about the kind of success that Jean-Paul embodies within the context of a Zafimaniry village. According to traditional Zafimaniry ideology outlined above, the successful ideal fulfilment of life is the ability to transform oneself into a house that will become a village. Having numerous progeny is the prerequisite for such a transformation, but is insufficient in itself. This progeny must be successful but also be retained around the original house. It is in this way that one "becomes" a village. By contrast, the particular nature of Jean-Paul's success had resulted in two of his children leaving the village for another world, the urban "modern" world. They returned extremely rarely. His other two children remained in the village, but they were not particularly successful, and one had borne only one child. So from the traditional point of view Jean-Paul was a relative failure. The weakness of his position as a progenitor explained the ambiguity of his political status in the village. Jean-Paul was respected, and always represented the village to the outside, especially to the administration; but he was not powerful within the village because he lacked descendants. His house was not beautifully carved, but instead had a tin roof and had been heavily consolidated with cement: materials that he had obtained through his church contacts.

All this meant that when his Christian name was used, the attitude of speakers had to be placed somewhere along a continuum, one end of which was respect for Jean-Paul's achievements in the national world, the other end of which emphasized his relative failure inside the village. This ambiguity was also tinged with a feeling of betrayal and even hostility toward the subversion of values that the modern world implies. This is what explains the occasional irony. Every use of the name evokes a position somewhere along this continuum and constitutes a minute act of political philosophy. Nothing shows this better than what happens in meetings of the village elders. Jean-Paul is obviously included in these meetings, both because of his standing in the outside world and because of his standing inside the village that, though lower than his age and genealogical status would normally confer, is nevertheless considerable. What the elders most want to create in such meetings is a feeling of community and unity. So, on these occasions, they always abandon everyday village practice and address Jean-Paul by his teknonym. This not only marks him as an insider but also places him within the genealogical framework that explains the unity of the village and ignores the external divisive aspects that his baptismal name brings to the fore.

Conclusion

In a Zafimaniry village representations flicker on and off, evoked by communicative acts through which mental attempts to communicate representations and attempts to imagine the representations of others criss-cross. The evocations are given life in a multitude of ways, some linguistic; others not. Among the linguistic evocations are speech acts involving names. This multitude of evocations is neither chaotic nor completely predictable and organized. The degree of order is the product of shared socialization and the unification that comes from continuous interaction. The degree of disorder comes from different educational and life experiences, various patterns of interaction, and personality differences.

Of the partially shared orders that seem to emerge from the interactions in which names occur, three images seem particularly important. First, there is the image of the growing "social" person who achieves immortality through becoming a thing and then a place. Second, we have the image of the sensuous individual monad seeking satisfaction to a multitude of desires. Third, there is the imagination of a wider world of uncertain boundaries, which appears successively as Christendom, the modern world of nearby towns, the nation, or an even more global entity. All three images are fairly unstable, but the first two usually though by no means always appear in a temporally ordered relation whereby the first replaces the second in a process of depersonalization and ultimately dehumanization.

It would, therefore, be quite misleading to look for such a thing as a "Zafimaniry naming system." If system there is, it is the total system of village life that exists through a multitude of individual acts, of which linguistic acts are a significant element. It is a social system, but quite different in nature from the "social" evoked in communication. Furthermore, as the case of baptismal names illustrates, the social system in both senses is not, nor ever has been, bounded by the village. Linguistic acts of naming have meaning insofar as they enable individual minds to guess how they will be understood by other minds. These acts, like all other acts, are carried out within a set of beliefs about how things are and are understood by others to be. But these institutional factors should not make us forget that each instance of use of names, or of any other word or sign, has an individual character that in turn explains the open-endedness, subtlety, and fluidity of such talk.

Notes

1. For a discussion of the value of individuality among the Merina that would apply equally for the Zafimaniry, see Bloch 1989.
2. For a somewhat similar system, see Needham 1954.
3. Childless people may be called by a pseudoteknonym such as "father of children," "mother of children," or "father or mother of Koto" when Koto is being fostered by them. Such usages are, however, recognized to be mere polite euphemisms. The refusal of the Zafimaniry to accept adoption or other forms of nonbiological filiation contrasts with what occurs in many other parts of Madagascar.
4. The children of a single mother are usually referred to as the children of her parents.

References

Astuti, R. 1994. Invisible objects: Mortuary rituals among the Vezo of western Madagascar. *Res: Anthropology and aesthetics* 25, 111–121.

Bloch, M. 1971. *Placing the dead: Tombs, ancestral villages, and kinship organization in Madagascar.* London: Seminar Press.

———. 1989. The symbolism of money in Imerina. In *Money and the morality of exchange* (eds) M. Bloch and J. Parry, 165–185. Cambridge: Cambridge University Press.

———. 1992. What goes without saying: The conceptualisation of Zafimaniry society. In *Conceptualising society* (ed) A. Kuper, 127–147. London: Routledge.

———. 1995. People into places: Zafimaniry concepts of clarity. In *The anthropology of landscape* (eds) E. Hirsch and M. O'Hanlon, 63–77. Oxford: Clarendon Press.

———. 1999. "Eating" young men among the Zafimaniry. In

Ancestors, power and history in Madagascar (ed) K. Middleton, 175–190. Leiden: Brill.

Cole, J. 2001. *Forget colonialism? Sacrifice and the art of memory in Madagascar.* Berkeley: University of California Press.

Coulaud, D. 1973. *Les Zafimaniry: Un groupe ethnique de Madagascar à la poursuite de la forêt.* Tananarive: Fanontam-Boky Malagasy.

Geertz, H., and C. Geertz. 1964. Teknonimy in Bali: Parenthood, age-grading and genealogical amnesia. *Journal of the Royal Anthropological Institute* 94(2), 94–108.

Graeber, D. 1995. Dancing with corpses reconsidered: An interpretation of "famadihana" (in Arivonimamo, Madagascar). *American Ethnologist* 22, 258–278.

Lambek, M. 2006. What's in a name? Name bestowal and the identity of spirits in Mayotte and northwest Madagascar. In *An anthropology of names and naming* (eds) G. vom Bruck and B. Bodenhorn, 115–138. Cambridge: Cambridge University Press.

Lévi-Strauss, C. 1962. *La pensée sauvage.* Paris: Plon.

Needham, R. 1954. The system of necronyms and death names among the Penan. *South-western Journal of Anthropology* 10, 416–431.

Njara, E. 1994. Le nom de personne chez les Malgaches de religion traditionnelle. *Droit et Cultures* 28, 209–224.

vom Bruck, G. 2001. Le nom comme signe corporel. L'exemple des femmes de la noblesse yéménite. *Annales, Histoire, Sciences Sociales* 56(2), 283–311.

5

Is There Religion in Çatalhöyük or Just Houses?

A Cautious Introduction

On what expertise can a social anthropologist draw that might be useful for the interpretation of an early Neolithic site such as Çatalhöyük in Anatolia? When facing such a question, the anthropologist must accept the uncomfortable fact that he or she has probably much less relevant expertise than the professionals already working, either directly or indirectly, at the site. Not only do archaeologists use wonderful techniques in order to obtain data from the remains they uncover but they also have been trained to interpret their findings with a good deal of theoretical sophistication, which is the fruit of the history of their discipline. Furthermore, they dispose of much more expert general knowledge about the geographical and historical context. They therefore know best how to squeeze interpretation from their material. The social anthropologist joining such a project will, if only because he or she is ignorant of the history of archaeology, run the risk of appearing a blundering amateur who, as amateurs often do, simply repeats the mistakes of the past that the discipline has painfully learned to avoid. Is a twenty-first-century social anthropologist let loose on an archaeological site not likely to behave like a nineteenth-century archaeologist in matters of interpretation? The risk is great. The amateur's temptation to attribute fanciful meaning to this or that aspect of the findings on the basis of undisciplined analogies is evident. Characteristic of such mistakes is the assumption that features, or objects, that look vaguely the same as those used by contemporaries must have had similar associations in the past.

In order to avoid the worst pitfalls of this sort of jaunt into another discipline, severe self-examination on the part of the anthropologist is required. He must ask himself these questions: What might I bring to the process of interpretation that others cannot provide? In what way can I avoid incompetent or misleading attributions of meaning? The answer must come from what he can pretend to know better than the archaeologists. In the case of the site at Çatalhöyük, I have two things to offer. First, a theoretical approach that I consider might be helpful even though it is not widely shared among anthropologists; and second, a detailed ethnographic knowledge of two contemporary societies and cultures in Madagascar.

The relevance of the ethnographic knowledge is, however, far from obvious. After all, two contemporary locations in Madagascar are very remote in time and place from early Neolithic Çatalhöyük. What relevance might my knowledge of the Zafimaniry, the small Malagasy forest group I have studied for almost forty years, have to the central Anatolia of 10,000 years ago?

There was a time in the history of the social sciences when answering such a question would have been easy. The reply would have run something like this. The people of Madagascar have a simple type of technology that can be equated with that of the inhabitants of prehistoric Çatalhöyük and so it is a fair guess that both places would have shared many ideas, values, and practices. This would mean that I could then project what I know of the Zafimaniry onto Çatalhöyük. The fallacy of such reasoning is by now familiar. First, necessary or even probable linkages between technology and such things as religious and kinship systems have proved illusory because of the complexity of human history, itself the product of the cognitive character of our species. Second, although the people of Çatalhöyük are quite probably my genetic and cultural ancestors (as they are ancestors of the majority of humankind), the forest people of Madagascar are not the remote ancestors of anybody. Their history and the changes it has brought are just as long as that of any other contemporary people. Indeed, the people of Madagascar are probably, like us, partly the cultural and genetic *descendants* of the people who lived in central Anatolia in the early Neolithic. Thus, any direct analogies between the Zafimaniry and Çatalhöyük on the basis of unanalyzed resemblances of this or that trait should be treated as superficial and anecdotal.

There is, however, some ground for thinking that a person with my training and experience might be of more help than any random body on the Clapham omnibus. If I propose that what I know for Madagascar suggests what may have also been true in Çatalhöyük, it must be because elements of what we find in Çatalhöyük are not only reminiscent of elements I find in Madagascar but also because in Madagascar these elements are part of a pattern for which it can be argued that the different parts of the pattern imply each other for general reasons. Furthermore, it is necessary to explain why this pattern will recur in unrelated places and times. These explanations must inevitably depend on the proposition of chains of causation that ultimately go back to the general characteristics of our species. This is a tall order. However, the suggestions I propose to make concerning the significance of not directly documented aspects of Çatalhöyük can have any legitimacy only if such causation can be proposed. The recognition of similarities *must be* accompanied by theoretical arguments that explain why one thing is reasonably likely to imply another for reasons that go beyond and do not depend on any specific cultural formulation. This is what this chapter will attempt to do.

One implication of this approach is that I shall take into account only those findings from Çatalhöyük that are part of recurring patterns and therefore suggest necessary connections among elements. A rather sad effect of this method is that I shall have to ignore nearly all the exciting finds that have made the site famous, and this in spite of the feverish stimulation they produce in me, as in everybody else. I shall have nothing to say of the lady (if she is a lady) flanked by the figures of two leopards, or of the plastered skull, or the more bizarre headless burials, the leopard's claw, and so on. I shall have hardly anything to say, in print at least, about the thought-provoking murals for which all sorts of extraordinary explanations have been proposed.

The reason is that all these things are one-off instances that can, therefore, not be associated systematically with other elements, while it is the *pattern* of association that makes ethnographic analogies potentially relevant. Instead, I shall concentrate on those aspects of Çatalhöyük houses that occur again and again because it is only the pattern of recurrences that can with any degree of assurance be linked to general reasons that might explain how and why such a pattern might arise.

Çatalhöyük Houses

One thing about Çatalhöyük is clear. For most of the period of occupation, it was a place where houses mattered. Houses mattered in ways that went well beyond their practical functions. The careful orientation of the different parts of the house together with the elaborate wall decorations all show that these were no casual edifices.

Furthermore, a specific aspect of these houses is emphasized. There seems good evidence that the continuity of a house was a major value. The period of occupation of houses in Çatalhöyük varies, but many were lived in for periods of up to a hundred years. Such long occupation implies continual maintenance, and this is very evident in many of the houses that have been excavated at the site. What is striking from the excavations is the emphasis on a type of maintenance that was clearly intended to keep the house unaltered through time. The continual re-plastering that in the end created such a thick covering illustrates this and shows the irony of the situation at the same time. This apparent stability was achieved, as is the case for life in general, through incessant movement. I assume the re-plastering was intended to, and indeed achieved, the maintenance of the original whiteness that would be rapidly threatened by soot from the fires. This "restorative" aspect went much further when copies of the original decorations such as painting and molding that would be obscured by the re-plastering were carefully reproduced on the new surfaces.

The investment in this activity would be heavy, and the aesthetic value of such an activity would have been inseparable from the ethical.

Equally significant as the maintenance of the state of decoration, the internal spatial organization of Çatalhöyük houses was unchanging and was restored when damaged. This means that the various activities that occurred in the space were made to appear as repetitions of the same activity because they occurred in the identically con-structed place. A stable layout framed the most important time-consuming activities of life, compelling them to be performed in largely identical ways, as is suggested by the skeletal modifications of the inhabitants. This immobile/mobile repetition implies not only a (partial) denial of the passage of time but also a concept of replacement of per-sons in the case of long-lived houses. The woman crouch-ing by the fire would not always be the same individual, but different women would crouch in the same place per-forming the same tasks with the same movements. This stability of roles would be not merely framed by the house but actually imposed on the inhabitants by its recurrent maintained structure. Thus, it is in the house rather than in the body of the living that the longer-term continuity of the society would reside.

What suggests most strongly the emphasis on continuity is the way house replacement occurred on identical sites. It is clear that houses were occasionally destroyed so that a new house could be built on the same site, but the new house was made a replacement for the old in a way that created an aspect of immobility. Repetition was obviously of great significance, as is shown by the fact that posts were placed in the same locations, and all the practical and decorative features were either transferred or reproduced. The destruc-tion of houses through intentional collapsing or fire would thus involve continuity rather than ending.

But it is not only their elaboration and their longevity that underscore the significance of houses in Çatalhöyük. It is also the absence of any other competing focus. There are no symbolic places for large communities to assemble; no great houses that might have been palaces, courtrooms, or meeting-houses. There are houses and that's it. It is as if all the meaning of social life were contained in the houses. Their prominence, their continuity, and their contiguity suggest a pattern that implies, on the basis of our present knowledge, what the whole of Çatalhöyük was like.

Zafimaniry Houses

The kind of emphasis on houses and their continuity that the findings in Çatalhöyük suggest is, for the social anthropologist, reminiscent of certain phenomena that led to the proposal that there objectively exists a class of societies that can be labeled "house based." Indeed, the existence of such societies and what we know about them have inevitably influenced the cautious guesses I ventured in the preceding section. Whether this is a risky procedure and how it might be justified is the main purpose of this chapter. However, before considering the matter more theoretically and in order to explain to the reader the temptation of seeing Çatalhöyük as a "house-based" society, I shall outline those points that are most suggestive by describing very briefly the situation among the Zafimaniry (for more detail, see Bloch 1995, 1999).

Among the Zafimaniry, it is evident that houses matter if only because of the fact that they are strikingly solid, elaborate, and decorated in a part of the world in which the houses of most other Malagasy peoples are flimsy, temporary, and plain. The sturdiness of Zafimaniry houses and the motifs that decorate them led UNESCO in 2004 to recognize the carving skills of this particular Malagasy people, originally intended to decorate posts, walls, and windows, as being of World Heritage significance.

These carvings are a celebration of the lasting hardness of the wood of which the houses are made. The emphasis on continuity is everywhere. The Zafimaniry house and its contents are oriented to the cardinal points, and the activities that take place within the house are therefore organized according to a stable pattern. This is standard in rural Madagascar, but the emphasis on fixed spatial organization is far more elaborated and celebrated among the Zafimaniry than elsewhere on the island. The maintenance and beautifying of the house is the most important kinship duty of the relatives of the householders. No greater offense to morality exists than to harm an important house (Bloch 1995, 1999).

Finally, the symbolical dominance of the house over any other possible symbolical foci is clear. There are meeting places in some Zafimaniry villages, but they are hardly noticeable, in sharp contrast to what is the case for neighboring groups. Most remarkable in the context of related Malagasy groups such as the Betsileo and the Merina, the Zafimaniry are little concerned with tombs that are famously the symbolical and aesthetic focus of the other peoples' "social."

In these general respects, the Çatalhöyük and Zafimaniry situations are similar but inevitably there are further aspects that we can know in the Malagasy case and only guess at in the Anatolian one. The permanency of houses is foremost in both cases and therefore contrasts with the transformability and replaceability of people. In the Zafimaniry case, it is thus not surprising that the house, instead of the tomb, is the place where one communicates with ancestors who are thought of, not simply as progenitors, but in an equally important way as previous householders. Perhaps the relation of the inhabitants of Çatalhöyük to the dead buried under parts of the floor in their houses implied the same sort of connection we find in Madagascar. We shall never know, but such a situation is found, for example, in another house-based society: Tikopia, thoroughly studied by Raymond Firth. Here an area of the house was used to bury the dead under the floor, and succession was more a matter of a link between present inhabitants of the house with that of previous householders buried under the floor than of kinship filiation (Firth 1936, 76).

Another key aspect of the Zafimaniry house is thought-provoking in the Çatalhöyük context. Zafimaniry houses are, above all, places in which couples exist. They are the place in which masculinity and femininity come together fruitfully. This is true of gendered activities and of the material side of these activities. Thus the Zafimaniry stress how a house brings together the hearth and the tools of the hearth associated with the creative, procreative, and transformative contribution of women and the house post associated with the creative, procreative, and nurturing contribution of men. This coming together in a joint enterprise is often rhetorically illustrated by the combination of the supports of the roof from either side of the main beam that require each other if they are to hold up the single structure that covers the house.[1] These are elaborate ideas that would be most unlikely to have existed in the same form in Neolithic Anatolia, but it seems clear that the Çatalhöyük house was also a locus of the coming together of a variety of creative and transformative activities that were probably gendered.

Toward Theory: House-Based Societies

These two very brief sketches, which can be supported by reference to existing publications on both places, may have convinced the reader of the possibility of a recurrence of a simple basic pattern. In any case it is the recurrence of this pattern in a number of places that has led to the development of the middle-level theory of "house-based societies."

The idea of house-based societies, *sociétés à maisons*, gained its modern expression in the work of Claude Lévi-Strauss (Lévi-Strauss 1979). Lévi-Strauss's idea can be understood only in the context of his vast and somewhat personal theory of social evolution. For Lévi-Strauss, the focus of the way ancient peoples represented to themselves the process of human life and its differentiation from that of nonhumans was through the need for exchange that the people of these early societies imposed on themselves. Above all, it was the exchange of spouses, made necessary by the existence of the incest taboo, which was the key to early human society. In these systems, symbolic social reproduction thus occurred in the space *between* exchanging groups. According to Lévi-Strauss, a shift then occurred in a period that the French anthropologist leaves unspecified, but which we can reasonably deduce from his work was the early Neolithic.

Instead of the locus of symbolic reproduction being created by the maintenance of lasting distance of nonetheless exchanging groups, it migrated to the achieved union in which the exchange created something new. The focus became the completed unit reproducing as a result of successful conjunction. This new creation, inevitably of a woman and a man, became in many cases instantiated in a material form: the house. This material form then took over the continuity of society from the abstract concept of repetitive exchange that had characterized what Lévi-Strauss calls "elementary structures." In this new form, reproduction is caused by conjunction *within* a totalizing building. As is typical of the work of Lévi-Strauss, we are not quite sure what we are dealing with. Is he talking of history or of the logical possibilities of systems? How does the theory relate to specific cases? This is a particularly thorny question because the ethnography he cites in support of his argument has struck the specialists as very oddly interpreted. Yet, as is again so often the case in

Lévi-Strauss's work, in spite of these obscurities the theory
has proved to be fruitful and illuminating in a number of
unexpected ways. First of all, the theory led many anthropologists to focus on the importance of the house. Second, it
encouraged scholars to explore the nature of the connection
between social organization and material culture. Third, it
encouraged high-level theoretical reflection about what had
previously been considered mundane activities such as cooking, cleaning, sleeping, and house building.

The scenario sketched by Lévi-Strauss is a "just so story"
for which there is very little evidence, but it has struck many
chords among anthropologists who have studied societies in
which houses seem to be the foci of the symbolic reproduction
of life and in which the very materiality of the building becomes an aspect of social reproduction. Before Lévi-Strauss's
work on house-based societies, there had been ethnographies
for societies in which the architecture of houses seemed to
express the core values of the people concerned (e.g., Cunningham 1964; Littlejohn 1967). However, it was as a direct
result of the inspiration of his writing that in 1990 a group of
anthropologists got together to pool their specific knowledge
of a number of very varied places in order to explore what
reality might be given to Lévi-Strauss's speculations. The
meeting led to an edited collection, *About the House* (Carsten
and Hugh-Jones 1995), which brings together a variety of
cases, including that of the Zafimaniry, occurring in very different parts of the world. These cases loosely link up one with
another through certain themes, many of which had been
predicted by Lévi-Strauss. It thus became possible to argue
for the existence of "house-based societies" as a phenomenon
that transcends the specificity of locality and time.

The common themes that recur in the various ethnographic examples examined in the Carsten and Hugh-Jones
edited book have already been touched on in the discussion
of the Zafimaniry houses. They seem also to be applicable to
Çatalhöyük because they are entailed by the simple fact of
houses being the main or the only focus of the representation of social continuity.

Houses are places in which a range of activities takes place
and they are generally adapted so that particular activities
occur in particular dedicated parts. This is inevitably the
case for an activity such as cooking, which is exemplary.

This being so, a temporal dialectic is established between the actions and the place allotted to them. For example, although cooking occurs only some of the time, and who cooks and what is cooked will vary, the hearth remains in time the materialized, abstracted, and stabilized location of cooking irrespective of circumstances. The material hearth can thus be said to be similar to an abstract "concept" in the way that the concept indicated by the word "cat" is an abstract concept with a complex relation to the multitude of specific animals, existing in the infinity of specific times, to which it can legitimately refer. The hearth is thus a kind of concept for indicating both the actual activities and the social relations that make these activities possible.

It is this simple connection between the reality of cooking events and the "hearth" concept that explains the latter's meaning. Such a relation is much more powerfully determinant than would be conveyed by the idea of "symbolic meaning," which always implies an arbitrary signifier/signified relation, as in the old and very misleading semiotic model. Further elaboration may be built up on the "concept" base of the hearth, but it will always depend on the fact that the concept depends on the reality that cooking is done there although concept and activity are phenomena of radically different orders. The hearth is a concept, but it is a motivated concept and this applies in a similar way to the "concept" house. In the case of the hearth, any further accretion of meaning will always be partially determined by the universal human activity of cooking, by the physical characteristics of fire, by the chemical transformation of matter exposed to heat, and so on. This is why it makes sense to talk of "house-based societies" as a natural category; it is why there are recurrences in the significance given to houses, although every case of the concept will have unique aspects, and why it is therefore not unreasonable to hazard a guess at what was going on in Çatalhöyük. It is also why the word *symbol* as commonly used in the social sciences is so misleading because it suggests a lack of motivation.

The situation with cooking applies to other aspects of houses in house-based societies. Houses in most house-based societies are not only places in which cooking and eating take place but are also usually, though not universally, places in which couples are established and reproduce.

This is consistently an essential part of what houses are about. Again and again certain parts of the house are seen as female and others as male. However, in these particular types of societies it is the *conjunction* of these two aspects that matters and that makes the house the core of social reproduction. This is what Lévi-Strauss meant when he contrasted "house-based societies" with those societies in which it is exchange between descent groups that has the socially reproductive function. However, just as cooking maintains life processes, so too the fertile conjunction of male and female that the house "houses" has a motivated relation to the actual processes of reproduction. By their very materiality, the houses stabilize, and to a certain extent transcend, the very temporality of these processes.

Concepts are now understood to have at their core related theories about the world. This is true of houses in house-based societies and a key theory of the concept house in house-based societies, also motivated, is the "theory" of social continuity (see Medin and Wattenmaker 1987). The motivation of the "concept" makes possible a situation, such as occurs among the Zafimaniry, in which the houses of forebears and their continuing beauty indicate the promise of the continuing fertility of the offspring, the offspring of offspring, long after the originator's death.

One can go even further. Houses in "house-based societies" are usually situated within groups of houses. These groupings of houses must, if the "concept" of houses is charged in this way, create derived "concepts" that can indicate a wider social system based on locality and contiguity, but whose conceptual core nonetheless remains houses.

The work of Lévi-Strauss, together with Carsten and Hugh-Jones's edited collection, therefore suggest a recurrent pattern that, given the indications that have been unearthed, might well have occurred in Çatalhöyük. This is because the notion of house-based societies can be grounded in things about the world and about our species that motivate the meanings houses can be given. This motivation is what makes it probable that the historical path that has led to the specific formulations we find in different places and different times will have been taken, time and again, in the history of humankind without necessarily any kind of contact between the empirical instances.

Such a conclusion gives me some hope that, as a social anthropologist, I can make a better-informed contribution to our understandings of what might have gone on in Çatalhöyük than someone who attributes what has been found to the influence of little green men from Mars. There is, however, another element, underpinning the all-important motivation of the form "house-based societies," that applies to the great majority of human societies and that, although much more general, explains why human societies might be tempted again and again to take paths *of the sort* of which house-based societies are one, and only one, example.

Why Humans Might Be Tempted to Create House-Based Societies Again and Again

In order to theorize at this much more general level it is necessary to focus on a key characteristic of all human societies: they are built on representations of their continuity in time that transcends the moment. Such a representation is to a certain extent counterintuitive in that the empirical appearance of human beings and their interaction involves continual movement, incessant change, and constant modification. The representation of the social as permanent therefore requires a cognitive feat of imagination. It is the need for a foundation of some sort for this feat of imagination that leads to the appropriateness of houses as concepts on which a particular take on the social—the transcendental—can be built.

In what follows, I summarize a programmatic article written in 2008 (reprinted as Chapter 2 in this volume). There are many aspects of the social organization of animals closely related to our species such as the chimpanzees or bonobos that are reminiscent of human social organization. In all three species, there is continual politicking and competition for power, rank, and alliance. This side of things I call the transactional. However, there is, at least, one fundamental difference between nonhumans and us. Humans phenomenologically create what have been called roles and corporate groups. These have an existence that transcends the particular people who are endowed with the roles or who belong to the groups. What I mean by "transcend" is that these roles and groups seem to exist independently of people and on a very different time scale (Gluckman [ed] 1962). The role of king, for example, is famously separate from the holder, and this is made evident by the fact that one becomes a king through being given certain material paraphernalia that is said to "embody" the kingship: such things as scepters, stools, crowns, and so on. Corporate groups such as clans or nations similarly seem to have a life of their own, of which temples or origin sites are indications. Thus, although they may involve many people, they are often said to be one body. They survive irrespective of the birth, death, or other transformations of their members. These aspects of the social can be said to be transcendental in that they seem to negate the empirical flux of life.

Because the transcendental social implies a "life" beyond that of people, it involves a complex game with time. People are in a continual state of flux as are the relations that exist between them; this is the transactional phenomenology of the everyday. The transcendental social, however, appears as possessing great stability. This is true of roles that in extreme cases can ideally be passed on unchanged from person to person. Groups can appear to have extraordinary continuity, so it is possible for members of a clan to say such things as "we came to this country 300 years ago," even though it is obvious that this cannot be true of the speaker, his addressees, or the other living referees of the word "we." Furthermore, roles and corporate groups link up to form patterns, which some earlier anthropologists called, somewhat misleadingly, "social structure." This largely invisible transcendental social, separate from people and the strategies of their everyday lives, is altogether absent from the social of animals other than humans.

One obvious question about this transcendental imagination concerns how it is given phenomenological reality. Probably the most important mechanism for doing this is ritual. It is, of course, one of the most widely recognized facts about rituals, such as initiation rituals, that they "create" roles or membership of corporate groups. The theory of rites of passage has always stressed this. One "becomes" a member of Christendom through baptism or one "becomes" a knight through the ritual placing of the sword.

Another familiar point about such rituals is that they require, in their initial stages at least, a removal of the individual from the ordinary world of continual modification and transaction toward the transcendental world of roles and corporate group membership with its apparent fixity and stability. Thus, initiation rituals typically begin by separating people from the mundane world, as van Gennep and Turner both stressed (van Gennep 1960; Turner 1969).

It is worth noting why ritual in general removes people from the everyday. Human interaction of a normal sort, as with language, depends on the mutual reading and adjustment of intentionalities (Grice 1982; Sperber 1986). It is our continually modified and adjusted understanding of others that governs our interpretation of their actions or of their words. This continuous, ever-changing flux is what is denied in the transcendental world of roles and corporate groups, and it is not surprising therefore that one of the principal aspects of the usual meaning of the word *ritual* is that it makes intentionality impossible to locate (Humphrey and Laidlaw 1994; Bloch 2004). This is because ritual defers intentionality in the sense that the imagined originators of the actions or of the sounds of ritual (be they words or otherwise) are not the actors or speakers themselves. These latter defer to others, in the sense that they *follow* those who showed them how to act or speak in ritual circumstances. If they were the intentional originators of the forms of words and actions used, these words and actions would not be ritual. Ritual thus leaches out intentionality and the tumult of a life continually created by actions to make a static world in which roles and corporate groups can exist. This is the transcendental social.

But there is also another way in which the invisible imaginary world of the transcendental social can be given some phenomenological reality: through the material culture associated with it. This material culture can serve as the visible trace of the invisible transcendental. To return to examples used previously, crowns and thrones remain as the visible trace of the rituals when the transcendental that was ritually instantiated has disappeared. These objects may well have been created for the ritual and the transcendental; this is the case for crowns and scepters. But the same function can also be performed by material things, which have a quite other raison d'être, but that may be incorporated into ritual because they lend themselves to such use. A common example is landscape. For instance, the landscape that plays such a central role in Australian aboriginal rituals, while obviously far more than ritual, becomes ritualized and an anchor for the permanent social (Morphy 1995). This, however, requires that it be transcendentalized into a "concept" that exists beyond its empirical manifestation.

This is what happens with houses in "house-based societies," or with parts of them, such as the hearth. Obviously, houses have a practical side in these societies, but they are also made to vanquish time and thus become "concepts." They then can be seen as a visible residue of the transcendental social and the rituals that bring it to life. However, the relationship between the transactional and the transcendental sides of the house is closer and more complex than that between the Australian landscape and aboriginal ritual. This is because, as discussed previously, houses are sites of continual activities at the same time as they become stable points in the system of the transcendental social. This both denies the fluidity of the house process and draws its meaning from it. The transcendental cannot be separated from very common universal human practical activities.

So the reason why the anthropological record can be used with a certain degree of confidence for suggesting what happened in Çatalhöyük is because house-based societies are doubly motivated. The reasoning goes like this. We can assume that, like all human societies (there are a few doubtful exceptions), Çatalhöyük society involved a transcendental time-denying social element and that this required support. Such a support very often involves a material manifestation of the invisible transcendental social. A readily available way of using the material world to express the invisible transcendental social is the house because houses, by their very nature, lend themselves to the representation of a continuity that transcends the moment. They and the activities that go on in them readily become concepts and as such are suited to the purposes of the transcendental social. But the concepts so created are not arbitrary, but linked to the practical. The concept houses in these societies are determined both by the universal needs of the transcendental and of the transactional and practical that take place in them.

The repetition of pattern that we find in a house-based society is thus the product of a not necessarily universal but frequent causal chain that ultimately derives from a particular combination of a number of generic human characteristics. Thus, what went on in Çatalhöyük can be illuminated by what goes on in Madagascar and in other places with house-based societies because the category "house-based societies" is a recurrent phenomenon repeatedly engendered by a combination of generic factors.

Dangerous Further Steps

Can we go further? So far, very little information from the Çatalhöyük finds has been used in the argument for reasons outlined at the beginning of this chapter. In this final part, I shall take greater risks by considering another recurrent characteristic of Çatalhöyük houses: the aesthetic deployment of strong wild animals, particularly cattle, which is evident in the use of bucrania on walls and in the occasional pictorial representation of scenes such as the famous "bullfight."

In Çatalhöyük there seems to be an emphasis on wild animals in decoration and a significant neglect for this purpose of domesticated animals, especially of sheep. This is surprising given that domesticated livestock existed at the period and must have represented an important economic asset. On the basis of this fact and the seeming preference for using nondomesticated animals in aesthetic contexts, I propose that two aspects were probably prominent in explaining these choices. One is the strength of the wild animals and possibly their virility, perhaps exemplified by the horns that are prominent in Çatalhöyük and that often have this symbolic role.

Second, is the fact that these strong beasts have been mastered and killed, perhaps in *corrida*-style slaughter.

These somewhat tendentious proposals are again influenced by my knowledge of the ethnography of other parts of the world and must, therefore, also be justified in terms of motivated meanings, in the way that I have done previously.

In order to make my argument, I refer briefly to the theory I outlined in the book *Prey into Hunter* (Bloch 1992). In that book, I argued that the phenomenological creation of what I have called the transcendental social always creates a metaphysical problem. The transcendental social requires a ritual removal from the transactional in order to construct an invisible world of roles and groups within which people act some of the time. This removal inevitably implies a movement out of life and vitality because the world of the transcendental is not one of transformative beings. This leads to the dramatic acting out in rituals of what I have called "rebounding violence": the dramatic reconquest of vitality in a conquered form that then "reanimates" the transcendental. Rituals that have been called sacrifices often display this element but so do many others.

Reanimation ideally involves the absorption of vitality, and contact with large strong animals is often used for this. These animals may be domesticated, but in that case they are often re-represented as wild. This is the case in Hispanic *corridas.* The general reason for this is that wildness is associated with untamed nondomestic strength. Often, however, the animals are wild in the first place; for example, the lions used in Roman sacrifices.

Using this theory, I would *very tentatively* suggest that the prominence of wild cattle in Çatalhöyük houses is to be explained in the following way. Houses, as we have seen, are probably anchors for the disembodied transcendental, but the ritual creation of this image requires a negation of the fluid changing aspects of transactional life. To create the houses of house-based societies, the continually changing phenomena of living things need to be ritually removed. This is evident in the first stages of initiation rituals mentioned previously. Thus, the phenomenologically stable, time-defying "concept" house replaces the fluid ephemeral life of people and their activities. The ethereal transcendental house so created then requires ritual reanimation. The reanimating element must be subordinated to the house; otherwise the house's very existence would be threatened by it. Thus the strength must be returned, even emphasized, but *only* in a conquered, controlled form. The dramatic introduction of conquered and killed wild cattle, and probably the consumption of the flesh, would then be the reintroduction of vigor and life-in-time to the house. The bucrania would thus either achieve this revivifying of the transcendental or celebrate moments when it occurred in sacrificial-like rituals.

What about Religion?

The Templeton initiative that led to the publication of the book in which this chapter first appeared was about religion at Çatalhöyük, yet my chapter has not mentioned the word once.

This is no accident. The reason is that I am confident that there was no religion in Çatalhöyük, any more than there was religion among the Zafimaniry before Christianity arrived there. Looking for religion is a wild goose chase. The English word *religion* inevitably refers to what English speakers have known as religion, and no amount of redefinition or manipulation of the term can escape the associations of this particular history. It is clear that calling the phenomena usually indicated by the words *Hinduism* and *Buddhism* "religions" has similarly led to misunderstandings (Fuller 1992). The kinds of phenomena that the English word *religion* and the associated word *belief* can be made to evoke have, at most, a history of 5,000 years. This dates to thousands of years after the establishment of Çatalhöyük. I have tried in an earlier chapter to suggest the processes that might have led to the creation of religion, and how these processes inevitably made use of pre-existing cultural and cognitive phenomena (see Chapter 2). These pre-existing elements have to do with the nature of the human social and could have been used for a host of other developments. Some of them are found in a specific form in house-based societies, which is why I have talked of houses, roles, corporate groups, and the transcendental rather than about religion.

Note

1. The house supports must be even-numbered on one side because even numbers are associated with males, and odd-numbered on the other side because odd numbers are associated with females.

References

Bloch, M. 1992. *Prey into hunter: The politics of religious experience.* New York: Cambridge University Press.

———. 1995. The resurrection of the house among the Zafimaniry. In *About the house: Lévi-Strauss and beyond* (eds) J. Carsten and S. Hugh-Jones, 69–83. Cambridge: Cambridge University Press.

———. 1999. "Eating" young men among the Zafimaniry. In *Ancestors, power and history in Madagascar* (ed) K. Middleton, 175–190. Leiden: Brill.

———. 2004. Ritual and deference. In *Ritual and memory: Toward a comparative anthropology of religion* (eds) H. Whitehouse and J. Laidlaw, 65–78. Walnut Creek, CA: Altamira Press.

Carsten, J., and S. Hugh-Jones. 1995. Introduction. In *About the house: Lévi-Strauss and beyond* (eds) J. Carsten and S. Hugh-Jones, 1–46. Cambridge: Cambridge University Press.

Cunningham, C. 1964. Order in the Atoni house. *Bijdragen tot de taal-Land- en Volkekunde* 120, 34–68.

Firth, R. 1936. *We, the Tikopia. A sociological study of kinship in primitive Polynesia.* London: George Allen and Unwin.

Fuller, C. J. 1992. *The camphor flame: Popular Hinduism and society in India.* New Haven, CT: Princeton University Press.

Gluckman, M. (ed) 1962. *Essays on the ritual of social relations.* Manchester: Manchester University Press.

Grice, H. 1982. Meaning revisited. In *Mutual knowledge* (ed) N. Smith, 223–243. London: Academic Press.

Humphrey, C., and J. Laidlaw. 1994. *The archetypal actions of ritual.* Oxford: Oxford University Press.

Lévi-Strauss, C. 1979. *La voie des masques.* Paris: Plon.

Littlejohn, J. 1967. The Temne House. In *Myth and cosmos: Readings in mythology and symbolism* (ed) J. Middleton, 331–356. New York: Natural History Press.

Medin, D., and W. Wattenmaker. 1987. Category cohesiveness, theories, and cognitive archaeology. In *Concepts and conceptual development: Ecological and intellectual factors in categorization* (ed) U. Neisser, 25–62. Cambridge: Cambridge University Press.

Morphy, H. 1995. Landscape and the reproduction of the ancestral past. In *The anthropology of landscape* (eds) E. Hirsch and M. O'Hanlon, 184–209. Oxford: Clarendon Press.

Sperber, D. 1986. *Relevance.* Oxford: Blackwell.

Turner, V. 1969. *The ritual process: Structure and anti-structure.* London: Routledge and Kegan Paul.

van Gennep, A. 1960. *Rites of passage.* Translated by M. B. Vizedom and G. L. Caffee; introduction by S. T. Kimball. London: Routledge and Kegan Paul.

◇

6

Types of Shared Doubt in the Flow of a Discussion

Doubt, as a philosophical subject, has traditionally been studied as a tool for the establishment of truth. This type of discussion involves controversies in which anthropologists generally find themselves out of their depth. More recently, however, many philosophers have abandoned such ultimate questions and have instead taken a naturalist approach to matters of truth and, therefore, also to matters of doubt. They have wanted to know what kind of psychological states are involved in knowing and doubting. They have also sought to analyze the basis of claims to truth that are actually used as they occur naturally. This has then led them to ask in what settings claims to truth are made. Do these different settings, especially different cultural settings, affect what is considered as true, and what are the ways truth can be claimed and validated? Similar questions can be asked of doubt.

The naturalist turn has thus, in the first instance, made philosophers into psychologists, but it would seem that it should also lead them to become ethnographers and anthropologists, or, at least, to consult ethnographers and anthropologists about what the latter have found and the conclusions they have reached. The reason is that mental states are not independent of the environment in which individuals live, especially the social environment. Doubt may be a solitary mental state, but it is often shared and, when this is the case, it is probable that a dialectic is established between the public manifestation of shared doubt and private internal states. To be complete, a naturalist philosophy of doubt therefore calls for an ethnography of shared doubt.

To a certain extent, a dialogue between philosophers, psychologists, and anthropologists regarding the ethnography of truth has begun to happen, though, for various reasons, it has also proved to be frustrating for the different participants.[1] However, as far as I am aware, no such exchange has occurred regarding doubt. This is probably because, at present, the ethnography and the anthropology of doubt hardly seem to exist.

The absence of an ethnography of doubt is not an accident, but seems to be due to a fundamental difficulty. Unlike knowledge and truth, doubt is rarely a subject for explicit argument or reflection. This difficulty can, however, be turned into an advantage. The ethnography of truth has for the most part concentrated on folk epistemic *theories* whereas it should have concentrated equally, if not more, on epistemic *practice* that occurs in the flow of social life. With the absence of similar folk theories of doubt, anthropologists have no alternative but to extricate doubt from what is occurring in naturally ongoing processes. This is what I do in this chapter by examining two instances of shared public manifestations of doubt while leaving to one side the difficult issue of the relation of these public manifestations to internal states.

The Setting

My main aim in this section is to distinguish two different types of shared public manifestations of doubt. For this, I turn to a consideration of a number of structured group discussions concerning Zafimaniry psychological theories that I organized in a small village in 2003.

The Zafimaniry are a group of forest dwellers in Madagascar who, for historical reasons, are relatively isolated and fairly distinct from other Malagasy peoples. A good deal of information about them has already been published (e.g., Coulaud 1973; Bloch 1995). Of significance here is the fact that in spite of the presence of a church school, the villagers can be considered as either unschooled or minimally exposed to schools because the school has hardly ever been in functioning order. Consequently, very few villagers, if any, are able to read and write efficiently.

This lack of formal education led me to ask what the villagers would make of a very academic psychological experiment that has been considered of great significance for our understanding of the cognitive development of young children. I wanted to place these unschooled villagers in the position that academic psychologists place themselves in when drawing inferences from experimental work and then compare the interpretations they made of the same phenomena (Bloch 2005). The experiment in question, which is usually called the false belief task, takes many forms. It is often interpreted in the literature as showing that young children do not understand that other people can hold false beliefs and that they therefore act honestly but mistakenly in terms of these beliefs. Because I discuss the findings of this research in Madagascar elsewhere in this volume (see Chapters 1 and 7) and intend to do so more fully in future work, here I shall only consider data that were, in many ways, minor byproducts of the main enterprise.

I was primarily interested in the villagers' interpretation of the false belief task, but I also used the discussions that followed the experiment as bases from which I could lead my interlocutors toward much more general reflections and speculations about mind, language, memory, dreams, ancestors, and so on. Here I am concerned only with parts of these extensions of the basic research and the unplanned speculative directions in which the villagers and I were led by the dynamics of the dialogue. These intellectual journeys on several occasions brought us to topics where the participants expressed doubt—although, as we shall see, not always the same type of doubt.

Two Types of Doubt in a Malagasy Village

Although I conducted a number of sessions of experimentation in the village, and some produced much longer discussions than others, all the discussions were surprisingly consistent. I therefore use as an example here only one such journey toward doubt that can be considered typical.

We had been discussing the relation of language to thought in people and I had discovered, somewhat to my surprise, that the Zafimaniry villagers shared a clear theoretical position on the question. The more vocal among them told me that thought and language were very different matters, and that language was not necessary for thought. It seemed from the general approval with which these statements were greeted that everybody agreed about this; there was no hint of doubt that I could detect among the small crowd that had gathered in the house in which the experiment took place. The only discordant voice was mine when I expressed a certain amount of disingenuous surprise bordering on skepticism. This attitude caused my interlocutors to want to convince me of their point of view, and for this they used the example of the deaf and dumb man who lives in the village and who, so they argued, was clearly capable of thought while at the same time being deprived of language. Indeed, people had often expressed great admiration for this man's ability to communicate. I was genuinely impressed by this example and the rhetorical use my interlocutors made of it, but I continued the discussion by raising another question. I asked whether animals, who obviously could not speak, were also capable of thought. Again, the answer was loud and clear: Yes, they were! In order to convince me of this, my interlocutors provided another example. They said that when pigs see someone come out of a house carrying a basket full of taro, they come rushing to the spot because they *think* that there will soon be peelings that they will be able to eat as they fall to the ground.

At this stage, I encouraged the joint intellectual journey to move yet further by asking whether this was the case for other animals such as chickens. The answer I was given was the same as that for pigs and similar examples were used to convince me that all animals could think. By then, however, the dialogue was becoming something of a joke because the question was being considered for ever more lowly animals. In the boisterous linguistic melée that was developing, some of my interlocutors adopted my part in the dialogue, not by taking my side of the argument, but by anticipating my next question only to answer it as soon as they had formulated it.

"What about fleas?" they asked, and their answer was "clearly fleas thought because they hid in the seams of garments so as not to get caught." This thought experiment delighted everybody, so I played my last card. "Do trees think?" I asked. The assembly became quiet and thoughtful, partly because trees are of central importance to the Zafimaniry and therefore not a joke. Most people said that trees could not think, but they did not argue the point. However, the participant who had most clearly enjoyed the intellectual game, an old friend of mine, ingeniously proposed the opposite of what seemed to be the general opinion and argued his point in the following way. "Yes," he said, "trees think, and this is shown by the fact that their roots, when finding themselves on rock, seek out the wet soil by growing towards it."

Did he believe that trees thought? This was not the interpretation I made of his intentional meaning. Basing myself on the multitude of pragmatic and contextual clues that framed this speech act as, indeed, they frame all speech acts, I believe he was saying this: "this is an intriguing possibility, and the line of argument we have been following could well lead to such a conclusion, but we have now reached a pretty ridiculous level of talk and I am not really committed to what I am saying." We had entered doubt, and I believe this mood of doubt was shared. However, this conclusion of mine is based only on interpreted micro clues, too impermanent to take in consciously and analyze, far less to describe. Such clues are the only evidence possible for the existence of this type of doubt in such a context. This is probably why the ethnography of doubt is so rare in the published record.

The ephemeral and inexplicit character of the phenomenon does not, however, mean that it is not worthwhile to reflect on what is involved. The best way to do this is to consider that this sort of doubt exists within a dialogic movement from certainty toward the unknown. This is what happened in the discussion I have outlined. During the early part of the interchange, the villagers seemed, as a group, certain of what was being asserted. Their certainty was based on a combination of two factors. First, it was based on their trust in the testimony of other people who had assured them in the past that things were so. Because of this and because of their trust in the opinion of others who were present in the room, people who either did not know this before, or more probably had never thought about the matter, were certain that pigs are capable of thought. Second, those who had been clear about the matter used empirical evidence, drawn either from their own observations or from the reports and interpretations of others, to support the received wisdom and make its propositions more convincing. The use of evidence from the senses, especially sight, is characteristic of Malagasy reasoning, as it is probably of reasoning in most places in the world (see Chapter 3). In this case, the empirical support provided by the reference to pigs anticipating food clearly did its rhetorical job successfully. The empirical evidence was not just left to speak for itself, however; instead it became a tool in a process of induction and deduction that led ultimately onto more dangerous and uncertain ground. This was ground more remote from the certain truth of the testimony that had been relied on and the truth guarantee that had been provided by relevant empirical evidence. Distance from certainty had moved the discussion to the territory of doubt. Believing that trees "thought" was not something people had shared in the past, and only one individual was now asserting it in a somewhat tentative tone of voice.

To understand the occurrence of this type of doubt, it is essential to place it in the developmental movement of shared thought. This is central for realizing where this doubt has come from and also for where it might be going. The villagers clearly enjoyed the perilous nature of the assertions they or others were making as they moved ever forward in their joint reasoning into less secure territory. Their attitude, however, also made it quite clear that at the same time as they were moving in this direction, they were also quite prepared, expecting almost, for their doubt to be dispelled in the future, either because of new testimony from others, whether present or not, or through the use of new empirical evidence. This type of doubt was thus seen as but a necessary moment in the exciting and, in this case at least, jolly progression toward firmer truth. This moment of doubt was therefore not all that dissimilar to the use of doubt as a key scientific tool advocated by a whole line of philosophers, Descartes perhaps being the most well-known among them.

The processual character of the type of doubt just discussed is particularly revealing in that it offers an instructive contrast to the second and very different type of doubt I consider next.

From the type of discussion reported here emerged the idea that thought is very much a matter of aligning intention and action for the Zafimaniry, and probably for most other Malagasy. They have a very pragmatic and down-to-earth approach to mind. I was therefore intrigued by how this could connect to other aspects of their culture, especially their relations to dead ancestors that had always seemed to me contradictory. Would I be able to move our discussions about questions of mind, which had been of a scientific character, smoothly onto these other matters that many anthropologists characterize as religious or mystical (Tambiah 1990)?

For a number of theoretical reasons that are not the subject of this chapter, I doubted whether this could be done. At first, however, I seemed to encounter few difficulties.

I began by asking about the mind in sleep. The Zafimaniry often make declarations and act in ways that the anthropological literature would normally label as ancestor worship. Thus, villagers make offerings to the dead to obtain their blessing. They fear the ancestors' displeasure. They believe that when this displeasure has been incurred, the dead manifest themselves to the living by asking for certain rituals to be performed for them. These demands are most usually made in dreams.

As was the case for the discussion on the first type of doubt, I use one particular conversation/experiment as an example. What was said in this one case was, however, very similar to what was said on the other occasions.

Discussion of the relation of sleep and mind started with my being told with great certainty and unanimity that in sleep one was "as if dead." After death, all activity stopped, and one was certainly not able to think. Similarly, in sleep the mind switched off and that was it. It seemed as if nobody present had any doubt about these matters. Although I had heard this sort of thing before, I found these statements nonetheless surprising in relation to both death and sleep because they seemed inconsistent with the beliefs and practices concerning ancestors. Rita Astuti, working in another part of Madagascar, has examined with great precision a similar apparent contradiction (Astuti 2007).

Because of the prima facie contradiction between the propositions just expressed and my knowledge of Zafimaniry ideas concerning ancestors, I asked the villagers about dreams and how, for example, it was possible for ancestors to come in dreams to ask to have a ritual performed for them if one was then "as if dead." The mood changed in a way that I cannot fully document empirically, but I am certain that it changed. In any case, the rather boisterous atmosphere that had characterized the discussion up to that point disappeared, and people became much quieter. I believe that the contradiction that lay behind my questions was sufficiently salient for a good number of people to understand what I was driving at, and that this is what explained the change of mood. Several villagers had already said by this point that in talking about dreams we were moving to an area that was "difficult."[2] However, I also got intriguing answers from two or three senior people. The most vocal of these put the matter in this way. "Although people who are asleep are like dead, the spirit of other people could come and be active in the sleeper's head." This answer does indeed remove the apparent contradiction that I had been exploring.

I could not tell with what degree of certainty this proposition was expressed, but the reaction of several other people was interesting. They approved what was being said by deploying one of several Malagasy equivalents of the English words *yeah yeah*, a vocalization that was accompanied by several semantically significant movements of the head. In this case, I assumed the meaning went something like "thank you, this matter is clear now that you have explained it." The explicit meaning of the nodding was that doubt had been removed, but it also implied a modification in the relation of discourse to fact. I interpret this as meaning that we have reached such a very difficult area in the dialogic process that neither evidence from the senses nor induction or deduction can be relied upon, so it is best to turn for information to authority figures who can be trusted. What made this clear was the contrast between this particular stage in the discussion and what had gone immediately before, as well as the mood that had characterized the previous discussion about the mental capacity of animals. All kinds of people had joined in these earlier discussions: women and men, old and young (with the possible exception of young newly in-married women). Indeed, older women dominated in these more matter-of-fact exchanges. By the time we moved to the discussion about dreams, however, only senior male author- ity figures spoke, and the other people present expressed deference to their opinion.

As a good rationalist, I pushed the discussion further, asking more and ever trickier questions about the spirits of the living and of the dead and the way they manifested in dreams. For example, I said (untruthfully) that the night before I had dreamed of my son, who everybody knew was alive, and asked whether that meant that he had somehow come to me from England. The mood caused by this type of question was totally different from the enthusiastic and somewhat amused explorations of such questions as the minds of pigs. People were uncomfortable, and I was told somewhat sententiously that these matters were too difficult and that one could not be sure. We were back with doubt, but with a very different type of doubt.

Another revealing event occurred during this discussion about dreams and spirits when a respected older man from a nearby village, who just happened to be passing by, came and joined us, probably intrigued by the gathering. People explained what was going on and asked his opinion on the questions we had been discussing. On many points he con- tradicted what had been said, but nobody pointed this out and he was heard with respect. It is not possible to discuss here the many issues he raised. I suspected at the time, and still do, that he was making up theories on the spot in order to impress. In particular, he asserted that the spirits that came in dreams were not *fanahy* (the word normally used and the one we had employed up to then), but *ambiroa*. I was not, and am not clear to this day, whether he meant that a different kind of entity was involved or that the proper name for the same entity was *ambiroa*. What is sure, however, is that his views on this and other matters were either esoteric or at least heterodox because *fanahy* is the word normally used in the village, as indeed generally in Madagascar, al- though people also sometimes talk of *ambiroa*.[3]

In spite of the oddity of what he was saying and the fact that he was contradicting what had been said and approved shortly before, the reaction to his views was very similar to the way the views of the other elders had been received.

Again people nodded and said *yeah yeah*, implying that they had learned something new and of great value. The flat contradiction with what had been previously said was left in suspension, as it were. It was not that the new actor in the discussion had imposed his view because, in spite of the expressed approval, as far as I could see everybody carried on talking about *fanahy* after his intervention. What I believe happened is that we had reached a type of discourse characteristic of a topic that was in doubt.

This doubt is a fundamentally different type from the doubt expressed on the question of whether trees could think, however. There was nothing to be done to remove it. The approval that had been expressed following what the senior men had said turns out, on reflection, to be much less straightforward than I had initially taken it to be. It was not a matter of believing that after their intervention we now knew what things were really like. If that had been the case, the contradictions between the village elders and the passing incomer would have caused confusion. What I now think was being expressed was something like this: "We are in an area in which we are in doubt and where we shall remain in doubt. Those in authority are expressing an opinion, but we cannot pass judgement on their opinion because we are in an area beyond our competence. We listen to them with respect, but that does not remove our doubt, nor should it."

Conclusion

In one of the rare anthropological discussions of shared doubt, Dan Sperber criticizes those writers who remove the element of their informants' doubt from their ethnography (Sperber 1982). There is indeed a tendency among anthropologists to try to push informants to explain things until they become clear and categorical, thereby obscuring the equally important ethnographic fact of the presence of uncertainty. Sperber quite rightly shows how misleading this can be with an example from his own field experience concerning a request by an old man for him to kill a dragon. Sperber argues that it would be tempting to conclude from such a request that the Dorze of Ethiopia believe straightforwardly in the existence of dragons; instead he suggests that the reality was that the old man was in doubt about the existence of dragons and was merely "floating" the possibility.

This discussion is extremely useful, but I am less sure that trying to specify the character of the propositions made is necessarily the best approach. In the preceding examples, I would not know exactly which Zafimaniry statements I would qualify as "semi-propositions," to use Sperber's term. It is as stages in the process of the exchange of words and actions that doubt comes to the surface and that its significance becomes clear. The contrast between the types of doubt illustrated here is above all a contrast in the character of dialogic moments that lead to different types of sharing of doubt. These inevitably lead to different types of dialogic developments that in turn lead to different future reflection and action.

Both cases discussed here evoke the word *doubt* as it is normally understood in English, and perhaps both involve similar internal states. But if we put them within the context of the social and linguistic flow in which they occur and are shared, they have little in common. In the first case, the sharing of doubt is part of a dialogic process that encourages a joint quest for truth. Doubt is thus a tool to stimulate a forward movement. In the second case, we seem to be dealing with a growing agreement among ordinary people not to try to resolve doubt but to stay bathing in it and to delegate to authority the active search for truth, perhaps because one fears where such a quest might lead. In the second case, doubt is not a matter of forward movement; it is a device for stopping it.

In some respects, the contrast I am drawing corresponds to the traditional contrast between science and religion that many anthropologists and philosophers have noted (Tambiah 1990). The problem is that both *religion* and *science* are terms that differentiate human social practices by their institutional characteristics rather than by the modes of reasoning they involve. Thus Keller demonstrates the use of "scientific" type reasoning among Seventh-day Adventists, people who would normally be thought of as engaging in religion (Keller 2005). Latour demonstrates the presence of doubt of the second type in "scientific" institutions (Latour and Woolgar 1988). It seems more fruitful then to examine the epistemic basis of discourses as they occur without allowing arbitrary labeling to obscure what we find.

Notes

1. See, for example, the discussions that followed the books edited by Wilson 1977 and Hollis and Lukes 1982.

2. The word used was *sarotra*.

3. Although several anthropologists and others, including me, have learnedly attempted to distinguish between *fanahy* and *ambiroa* (and several other terms), I now believe that we should have acknowledged that these words and the notions to which they allude are not clear, either to us or to our informants.

References

Astuti, R. 2007. Ancestors and the afterlife. In *Religion, anthropology, and cognitive science* (eds) H. Whitehouse and J. Laidlaw, 161–178. Chapel Hill, NC: Carolina Academic Press.

Bloch, M. 1995. People into places: Zafimaniry concepts of clarity. In *The anthropology of landscape* (eds) E. Hirsch and M. O'Hanlon, 63–77. Oxford: Clarendon Press.

———. 2005. Where did anthropology go? In *Essays on cultural transmission* (ed) M. Bloch, 1–19. Oxford: Berg.

Coulaud, D. 1973. *Les Zafimaniry: Un groupe ethnique de Madagascar à la poursuite de la forêt.* Tananarive: Fanontam-Boky Malagasy.

Hollis, M., and S. Lukes. (eds) 1982. *Rationality and relativism.* Oxford: Blackwell.

Keller, E. 2005. *The road to clarity.* New York: Palgrave Macmillan.

Latour, B., and S. Woolgar. 1988 (2nd ed). *La vie de laboratoire, la production des faits scientifiques.* Paris: La Découverte.

Sperber, D. 1982. Apparently irrational beliefs. In *Rationality and relativism* (eds) M. Hollis and S. Lukes, 149–80. Oxford: Blackwell.

Tambiah, S. J. 1990. *Magic, science, religion and the scope of rationality.* Cambridge: Cambridge University Press.

Wilson, B. (ed) 1977. *Rationality.* Oxford: Blackwell.

◇

7

Toward a Cognitive Anthropology Grounded in Field Work

The Example of "Theory of Mind"

The anthropologist's profession can certainly appear paradoxical. Those anthropologists with whom I feel a particular affinity—they include eminent practitioners who have had the honor of teaching within these walls (notably, Claude Lévi-Strauss, Françoise Héritier, and Philippe Descola today)—seem in the course of their careers to have engaged in two very different types of scientific inquiry. On the one hand, they devote considerable time and effort to acquiring detailed expertise on relatively tiny groups of people living in very specific places that they observe and then describe in their intimate singularity. On the other hand, these same anthropologists have no hesitation in making general and often extremely bold claims about the nature of human beings everywhere. In the first case, they pay meticulous attention to the infinite variety of human nature; in the second, they make the immense leap that is required to formulate general hypotheses about *Homo sapiens.*

Ethnography versus Theory

Not content with the pursuit of two such strikingly contrastive forms of inquiry, these same anthropologists often behave as if they were also quite determined, for some perverse reason, to maximize the disparities of scale. Committed to generalizing theory, they elect to conduct their ethnographic fieldwork in the most out-of-the-way places, places that the vast majority of us would probably dismiss as irrelevant backwaters of the swirling, globalizing world.

This curious situation is partly the legacy of a time when anthropologists believed that the relation between the two practices—ethnographic description and bold theorization—was fairly straightforward. Ethnography—for example, the study of a small group of hunter-gatherers, living in the depths of the Amazonian forest, with none of the comforts of modern life—was expected to furnish critical data for the elaboration of grand theories about the evolution of humankind. It was believed that the people dwelling in these remote places were living fossils whose ways of life and social organizations preserved those of the earliest stages of human history. Our contemporaries were treated for the purposes of evolutionary speculation as our distant ancestors.

No professional anthropologist today would entertain this type of evolutionary illusion. Yet there are still some anthropologists, among whom I count myself, who stubbornly persist in the discipline's bifurcated practice, but having rejected its original raison d'être, find themselves engaged in a scientific undertaking whose two foundations appear to have come adrift, throwing its center of gravity entirely off course. It is perhaps no wonder that when faced with an edifice under imminent threat of collapse, so many of my colleagues have abandoned anthropology's core duality to take up residence, so to speak, in one or other of the wings.

Some have chosen to be little more than ethnographers of one particular society. I am inclined to include within this category the numerous anthropologists who, focusing on modernity or captivated by globalization, have moved away from traditional field sites in order to conduct their investigations in very large research "localities" whose boundaries are often fuzzy and not easy to locate.

Other practitioners have made the opposite choice. Losing interest in the detail of particular places, they have become general theoreticians of society or culture. Their discourse is no longer inspired by the interpretative ethnography of a particular group of people, but instead takes the form of geographically unanchored abstract propositions that if they make any reference to particular ethnographies, they do so only for the sake of illustration. For these anthropologists, the day of the ethnographic monograph intent on capturing the rich detail of a particular social microcosm is long past. They continue, not without good reason, to define themselves as anthropologists, but they are not averse to sporting other labels. Often styling themselves by neologisms such as "evolutionary theorists" or "rational choice analysts," these anthropologists of the theoretician tendency have tended to drift away from traditional anthropology departments, abandoning them to the pure ethnographers.

I can well understand what prompts such reformulations of the subject matter of the discipline. At times, I, too, have been tempted to follow one or other of these two tacks. Nonetheless, in this and subsequent lectures, I will attempt a justification of anthropology as this dual and apparently incoherent undertaking that a number of us still holds dear. My primary concern here is not to rescue anthropologists from their largely self-inflicted cul-de-sac. The predicament of a particular discipline, however unfortunate, is, after all, in itself hardly a matter of great general interest. Rather, if I propose to argue the case for the practice of a bifurcated anthropology in this lecture, it is because I believe that its very special combination of highly localized fieldwork inquiry and general theorizing makes a distinctive and invaluable contribution to humankind's varied attempts to further our knowledge of ourselves.

To demonstrate how this might be possible, and, rather than plunge directly into epistemological arguments, I shall begin by describing very briefly the two kinds of research activity in which I engage and that I attempt to combine.

Ethnography

The first of my research activities is ethnographic. In recent years it has consisted in my travelling from Paris or London to the island of Madagascar where I participate for a while in the everyday existence of men and women who inhabit a small village deep in the tropical forest of the east coast. For nearly forty years I have been returning to this particular village, staying for periods of between a few weeks and a few months at a time, and I have written about many aspects of the villagers' way of life and how they think about their world. Why Madagascar? Because, when I was a student in the 1960s, it was exactly the sort of faraway, exotic destination toward which young anthropologists at Cambridge University, in search of a suitable location for fieldwork, were steered. I suspect the fact that apprentice anthropologists at this time were consistently encouraged to seek out the most distant places reveals the stubborn persistence of anthropology's colonial and evolutionist heritage, a past by then fiercely repudiated but that continued to haunt the discipline. And Madagascar at the time was a particularly intriguing destination because as a former French colony it had been little studied from within the social orientation of British anthropology. Why this particular village and not another? It is enough to say here that the choice largely came about for accidental reasons. And, finally, why have I continued to go there so regularly and over such a long period of time? In part, because—not without some difficulty—I have finally mastered the local language, and in part because I have come to know well the people who live there and I am very fond of many of them. A lasting bond has grown between us over time.

I readily confess, however, that, having visited the same place so often and become so familiar with the men and women who live there, I sometimes feel that there is little more I can learn about them and their society through traditional methods of ethnographic inquiry, which is not to say, of course, that another anthropologist visiting the same locality would not return with an infinite variety of new and interesting data to report.

Anthropological Theory: Types of Representation

The second kind of research activity that occupies much of my professional life is altogether different and may be called theoretical in the simple sense that I shall use the term in this lecture. By theoretical, I mean any research activity that attempts to say something about humankind in general. Thus, for a long time now, I have been interested in the issues raised by the coexistence in all human groups of different types of knowledge. This seems to me to be a central question for anthropology, and indeed for other human sciences, and it is a question that transcends any consideration of time and place. It concerns the relation between two different kinds of representation (verbalized or nonverbalized) that for the sake of simplicity can be thought of as two "sorts" of discourse that I shall contrast to the extreme, while recognizing that these two "sorts" are neither altogether unconnected in actual human experience nor fully separable from the analytic point of view.

One type of representation consists of well-rehearsed, almost proverb-like statements that are often expressed in ritual-like contexts. These representations are explicit and culturally highly variable. In much anthropological writing, representations of this kind have been treated, mistakenly in my opinion, as if they organized the cognitive life of the people concerned. Anthropologists have presented these kinds of data as if they unlocked the fundamental mental categories through which people belonging to this or that society perceive and interpret reality. One example of such an approach is Louis Dumont's thesis that the opposition between the pure and the impure constitutes the keystone of Indian cosmology (Dumont 1966).

By contrast, the other type of knowledge is normally implicit. It relies on the core knowledge that all human beings require in order to be able to make the continual and innumerable inferences that render everyday life possible, but also make it seem so unreflexive. This tacit knowledge—which is a knowledge that goes without saying—appears to be much less culturally inflected, as is demonstrated by the ease with which anthropologists generally manage to communicate and interact with the people they study, even in the most exotic of fields.

I began thinking about how to understand the simultaneous presence within every social group of these two different types of knowledge, and others, early in my career, and it has remained for me a subject of enduring theoretical concern. Over the years, I have pursued my interest in this question by reading widely in literature that treats directly or indirectly of the question and by participating in debates, through which I have sought to construct a well-argued point of view. I have taught courses on the subject and I have published articles. In short, in the course of trying to clarify the relationship between different kinds of human knowledge, I have engaged in the full gamut of activities that the general public more typically associates with academic life than sitting on a hillside in Madagascar, stripping maize cobs of their husks. Along the way, I have drawn on ideas and information from many sources: books, seminars, and lectures. I learned a great deal from the work of my teachers at the London School of Economics and at Cambridge (Raymond Firth, Meyer Fortes, Edmund Leach, and Stanley Tambiah). I have also benefited from the contributions of a number of other scholars, many of whom are French, such as Dan Sperber and Maurice Godelier; and several of whom have held chairs at the Collège de France (Claude Lévi-Strauss, Pierre Bourdieu, and Phillipe Descola), to name but a few of those who have taught me much.

More recently, however, like other anthropologists who remain deeply committed to constructing general theory, I have had to look increasingly outside the discipline, strictly speaking, for the conceptual frameworks and intellectual resources I need in order to explore my theoretical concerns. In fact, the more professional anthropologists have retreated from the generalizing aspirations of the discipline and dedicated themselves to ethnography alone, the greater my reliance on importing ideas and expertise from beyond anthropology has become.

The intellectual debts I have incurred to other disciplines in the course of my career can appear somewhat eclectic. Thus, I have found certain aspects of Marxist-inspired sociology very useful in my work, notably the critical distinction it proposes between ideology and practice. At the same time, I have been profoundly influenced by theories in semantics and pragmatics, deploying them as tools, not just for understanding everyday social interaction but also, more pertinently, for seizing the very special characteristics of ritualized action in contrast to more familiar modes of communication (Bloch 2004). Above all, I have drawn extensively on recent work in cognitive psychology, especially in developmental cognitive psychology, in order to understand the development and establishment of the tacit knowledge that human beings use in the infinity of ordinary inferences that organize their relation to the everyday world, and to ascertain the ways in which this kind of knowledge is culturally inflected. It is the centrality of this question to my ongoing research interests that leads me in this lecture to focus on asking how we might fruitfully combine two kinds of inquiry: the one—cognitive psychology—that claims to tell us about human beings in general, and the other—the ethnography of the specific—that deals with particular women and men.

To return to the question I posed at the very start of this lecture, why do I and some other anthropologists remain so attached to this two-sided practice combining theory and ethnography? It might seem at first sight a little curious if I were to suggest that repeated stays in a small Malagasy village help me to clarify the implications of recent developments in cognitive psychology and to assess the light they throw on the mechanisms of social and cultural life.

It would be tempting to try to justify the bifurcated character of my research practice and that of anthropologists like me, by borrowing from the model of inquiry familiar to scientists of all kinds. One might thus argue that one component of the anthropologist's work consists in the formulation of general hypotheses that the ethnographer—who is this self-same anthropologist—then tests against empirical evidence in the field. Unfortunately, if I reflect on my own trajectory since I first embarked on social anthropology in the 1960s, or if I consider the work of other anthropologists whose practice most resembles my own, I have to admit that no such straightforward scenario applies. In anthropology, in contrast to the classical model of scientific inquiry, it has never been the case of organizing a systematic and rigorous relationship between the theoretician's general propositions and the empirical data collected among particular men and women. Things do not happen that way. There has been no direct or simple link between fieldwork and theory, although the two types of research activity have interacted closely, of course, and each has enriched the other to some degree.

For example, when I drew upon ideas in the literature on semantics and pragmatics to analyze specific rituals in terms of their being a little like reported speech, this analogy helped me to recognize a dimension of social practices that I had previously overlooked (Bloch 2004). Similarly, the theoretical contributions of cognitive psychology led me to pay attention to certain features of everyday life in the Malagasy village that I would otherwise have missed (Bloch 1992). In particular, it was through my reading in the general psychological literature on memory that I became conscious of the dangers—to which the social sciences are so prone—of conflating the past that is recounted in narratives produced by social actors in the particular circumstances of public or collective life, with the knowledge of the past that is *stored* in the minds of individual human beings (Bloch 1998). Similarly, the literature on cognitive psychology inspired me to look more critically at a number of terms such as "agency," "identity," and "embodiment" that pervade the social science literature, and to ask precisely what psychological phenomena they are supposed to denote.

These are all very real advantages of the dual practice of anthropology. In themselves, however, they are hardly sufficient to justify the continuation of the present state of affairs. They show how theory can benefit from fieldwork and how fieldwork can benefit from theory, but they maintain the two practices as essentially separate and fail to make a sustained case for their fundamental and irreducible unity.

In this lecture, I propose to go beyond a view of anthropology as a discipline whose dual nature is an accident of its own short history to make the argument in favor of a view of cognitive anthropology as a generalizing project grounded intimately and irreducibly in fieldwork. I shall argue that the fruitful co-presence of these two types of research activity—ethnography and theoretical reflection—at the heart of the anthropologist's profession is not simply a matter of historical serendipity but instead an integral and necessary part of the discipline's approach. I shall suggest, further, that the value of contemporary anthropology lies precisely in its apparent internal incoherence and its double nature. Anthropology, at least as I conceive it, presents the immense merit of uniting knowledge about human beings—that is constructed from the top down, by general theory, which in the case of cognitive psychology is supported by rigorous and controlled experiments—with knowledge of particular men and women that is constructed from the bottom up, based on the observation of people as they live their lives. Further, it is my contention that anthropology contains an element of value for other human sciences. I would even wager that the need for such a combination of approaches is likely to be felt in a good many other disciplines, albeit in different forms.

Theory of Mind

To illustrate how the general principle of combining these two types of knowledge might work out in practice, I turn to a topic that has become a matter of speculation and research in a number of disciplines and with which I have been particularly concerned. The topic concerns the representation we make of the mind of self and others, and its role in the social process, a topic grouped loosely under the so-called "theory of mind."

Given the bifurcated kind of anthropology I have been practicing, it is perhaps hardly surprising that in the past I should have approached this subject in two very different ways. Thinking about "theory of mind" from the ethnographer's perspective, I have focused on what a particular group of Malagasy people have had to say about self and others as they went about their daily life. Thinking about "theory of mind" from the theorist's perspective, I have been more concerned with the general characteristics of the human species. However, a recent controversy has forced me to reconsider this dichotomous approach, and to think again about how these two ways of considering theory of mind might be reconciled. The controversy, in essence, turned on the relationship between ethnography and general theory.

In recent years a number of evolutionary scientists have convincingly argued that our large brain, the most significant of all our characteristics and the one that differentiates us most sharply from chimpanzees, developed not, as was previously thought, in order to enable us to resolve problems of a material or technological order, but rather as a tool for managing the complexity of human social life (Humphrey 1976; Dunbar 1992). They have made the point that human social life requires extraordinary coordination between people, and in order to coordinate with others, it is essential that we understand that they act, as we too act, in terms of internal mental states that we continually attempt to "read." A great deal has been learned in recent years about the development of this capacity for reading minds, thanks to advances in neurology (Frith and Frith 2001); through the study of its absence in autism (Baron-Cohen 2000); and in particular by observing the gradual development in children of the ability to understand the fact that they, and those with whom they interact, do not act in terms of how the world is, but rather in terms of the beliefs they hold about the world (Wimmer and Permer 1983; Gergely et al. 1995; Carpenter et al. 1998; Harris 2000).

This developmental process involves a number of key stages that appear to begin very early in the infant's life. In fact, the aptitude to acquire such a "theory of mind" is clearly given to us in the human genome; though, just like other capacities, it develops in specific contexts, and thus is influenced by factors both internal and external to the individual. Nevertheless, on the basis of work done thus far, it seems certain that the development of this capacity is only weakly affected by differences in culture (Avis and Harris 1991; Vinden 1999; Callaghan et al. 2005). It therefore would seem that our understanding of ourselves and of others, and, accordingly, of the nature of social relationships, is everywhere based on a fundamental, innate, and largely invariable capacity shared by all human beings.

Such an affirmation is likely to disturb, if not irritate, many anthropologists. After all, one of the most cherished assumptions of the discipline has been, at least since Marcel Mauss's famous essay on the category of the person (Mauss 1938) that this "category of the person," or of "the self," or the "I" (all distinguished in the most learned of ways), is culturally variable.

Ironically, in this instance, the somewhat predictable anthropological resistance to the growing body of work within the cognitive sciences on theory of mind was articulated, not by an anthropologist but rather by a scholar who is herself a psychologist by profession but who, for the occasion, has chosen to rely on the work of many social/cultural anthropologists. Thus, Angeline Lillard, with the support of myriad examples drawn from numerous ethnographies, argues that in many human groups the person and the mind are thought of in ways that differ radically from those one finds in the "West." She tells us, for example, that the Bimin-Kuskusmin of Papua New Guinea (studied by Poole in 1985) "view the mind as unknowable and unimportant" (Lillard 1998, 13).

The reader, confronted with such an extraordinary variety of concepts of the person, of the self, of the mind, or of social relations, can only conclude from Lillard's essay that representations of this dimension of human experience are infinitely plastic, and that in constructing "theory of mind," culture operates more or less free from any constraint.

If it was predictable that certain received anthropological wisdoms would be marshalled against the universalist claims of cognitive science, so too was the defense offered by those developmental cognitive psychologists whom Lillard had accused of ethnocentrism (Wellman 1998; Scholl and Leslie 1999). They have argued that the kind of evidence summoned by Lillard has no bearing on their own research findings because it is derived from the explicit statements of informants. By contrast, their argument goes, when psychologists describe "theory of mind," they refer to a cognitive capacity that ordinary people do not and cannot put into words. This is because—as Sperber (2000) among others has pointed out—the kind of ceaseless mutual monitoring of minds that is indispensable to social exchange involves simultaneous operations of such speed and complexity—I am reading your mind reading my mind possibly reading the minds of multiple others, and so forth—that these processes must occur below the level of consciousness, much as the brain regulates the beating of the heart. Following this line of reasoning, these psychologists have argued that the evidence assembled by Lillard from the work of ethnographers is inadmissible in the study of the psycho-social process of mind-reading. For the critics of Lillard, what anthropologists had derived from their informants' statements were at best meta-theories of theory of mind, held by various different people around the globe. But such meta-theories are ultimately irrelevant to the mechanisms at work in the kinds of communication that the psychologists were bringing to light. The implication was that psychologists could altogether ignore the kinds of data anthropologists/ethnographers collect and report from the field, and confine their analysis to a consideration of evidence produced in the course of laboratory experiments. And, in response to this kind of dismissive attitude, anthropologists have in turn tended to ignore the work of the psychologists.

There is, however, something profoundly unsatisfactory about this *cuius regio, eius religio* solution. It would seem to imply that human beings function on two totally unrelated levels, producing one set of data for anthropologists in the field and another set of data for cognitive psychologists in the laboratory. Moreover, it implies that what people actually say or do (which is to say, the kinds of thing the ethnographer hears or observes during fieldwork) is a kind of superficial crust, a disguise even, concealing a human reality of an entirely different nature—a reality that is unaffected by the historical phenomena that we commonly term *culture* and that is accessible only through laboratory experiments conducted in culture-free contexts. Such a radical dichotomization of human experience seems most improbable. And indeed it will be my argument here that any approach to theory of mind that starts from the premise of the existence of two totally distinct and incommensurate elements—the "conscious" and the "subconscious"—is fundamentally misconceived. For what is most important for our understanding of the specificity of human beings is precisely their seamless combination in real-life human contexts. After all, we know, if only from our own experience, that we are not these kinds of dual creatures that an unresolved incommensurability between the data produced by ethnography and the data produced by cognitive psychology would seem to imply.

It was in order to explore the relationship between these two types of data, instead of stressing their incommensurability, that I recently trialled a new research strategy in the field.

A Psychological Experiment in the Field

One laboratory experiment that has played a major part in enabling psychologists to advance their reflections on theory of mind is the so-called "false belief task" (Wimmer and Permer 1983). In one version of this experiment, children of different ages are shown a box of familiar candy, of Nestlé Smarties for example, with the brightly colored candy pictured on the sides of the box. Still in the presence of the child, but when its mother, or some other person, has left the room, pencils are substituted for the Smarties. The box is then closed and the child is asked what its mother will say when asked on her return what the box contains. Very young

children reply "pencils" while older children say "Smarties"—
as would, I imagine, most of the audience here today.

These sharply different responses have been taken to show
that first, the older child, unlike the younger child, under-
stands that people do not act in terms of how the world is,
but rather in terms of what they *believe* about the world; and,
second, that such an understanding is an essential element
in social interaction. Only once they have understood this
do children "pass" the false belief task. It is not my intention
here to discuss the vexed question of whether the ability to
"pass" this particular test in and of itself marks such a key
moment in the child's development. But there is no doubt
that the dramatic contrast between children who "pass" and
those who "fail" is an extremely powerful theoretical tool for
enabling us to think about the capacities that human beings
require for competent social action, and about the manner
in which these develop.

It was an appreciation of the potential of this simple
experiment to provoke reflections on fundamental human
characteristics and their development that led me to organize
a new kind of fieldwork in the Malagasy village I have told
you about. Thus I carried out a version of the false belief
task during my last research visit to Madagascar in 2004,
far from any laboratory and in front of any villagers who
were sufficiently interested to watch. The task was repeated
with a number of children of different ages with the intended
result that some would "pass" while others would "fail." My
concern, however, was not to study the cognitive development of village children. Rather, it was to listen to the way in
which adult villagers—in this case, adults with practically no
formal education and of whom only a few could just about
read or write—would account for the difference between the
children who "passed" and those who "failed." I hoped in this
way to discover new aspects of *their* theory of mind and of
their knowledge of child development.

The way I conducted the experiment was by using two lo-
cally produced raffia hats. In the presence of an adult, Koto,
sweets were placed under one hat. Koto was then asked to
leave the room, the sweets were switched to the other hat,
and the child was asked, "When Koto returns, where will he
look for the sweets?" As expected, the younger children indicated that Koto would look under the hat where the sweets

were now hidden while the older children indicated that Koto would look under the hat where the sweets had been placed before he left the room. At this point I turned to the adult audience and asked them to explain the difference between the younger and older children's response.

I had been rather apprehensive beforehand that the villagers would find the question at the very least unusual and show little inclination to discuss it, but I was soon proved wrong. With only minimal initial encouragement, the inhabitants of the village reacted enthusiastically to the intellectual challenge that interpreting the experiment and its results posed. Indeed, the series of experiments provoked animated group discussions, which in several instances lasted for well over an hour. In this short lecture I cannot begin to do justice to the rich data I obtained in the course of these discussions. I hope to report the findings in greater detail in future work. The crucial point to note here is that despite many areas of disagreement among villagers, a degree of general consensus on the core question of why the responses of the two groups of children differed nevertheless emerged.

In particular, nearly everybody agreed that the younger children, who thought that Koto would look under the hat where the sweets had been placed in his absence, did so because they had not yet developed the ability to *mandainga*. This is a Malagasy verb that I had previously understood as simply meaning "to lie." However, the extended discussions stimulated by the experiments soon revealed that this term in fact referred to a much broader human capacity, a capacity that villagers also sometimes indicated by the word *politique*—one of the very few French words they use. Politique, they explained to me, is what enables human beings to navigate our treacherous world in which people often say different things from what they actually believe, in order to further their own ends. A full account of what was said on this topic cannot be given in this lecture, but what became very clear is that what these unschooled Malagasy peasants were telling me was very close indeed to the conclusions academic psychologists and philosophers have drawn from the results of the false belief task. Namely, that, in contrast to young children, adults know that other human beings act in terms of what they believe about the world rather than in terms of how the world really is, and that it is this that, given the Machiavellian intentions that, unfortunately, characterize many of those with whom they have social relations, makes it possible to mislead others and to be misled by them.

Malagasy Villagers' Theory and Psychological Theory

The key point I want to draw from these Malagasy cognitive theories and underscore here is that there is no yawning gap between the information obtained from informants through ethnographic fieldwork and the general conclusions that the psychologists deduced from their laboratory experiments. If we put aside questions of style and language, the conclusions the Malagasy villagers drew from their observations of the experiment converge with those formulated by the psychologists. Given the battle lines that were drawn in the wake of Lillard's paper, this concordance should come as great a surprise for Lillard and the anthropologists she cites as for the psychologists whose theory of mind she critiques.

Why did the data produced on this occasion by this way of doing ethnography not reveal the same incommensurability with western scientific discourse that came to the fore in the discussions following Lillard's paper, a type of incommensurability that has been the subject of repeated controversy in anthropology and philosophy? Why, instead of uncovering distance, did I find convergence between scientists and Malagasy villagers on theory of mind? I would attribute this to two key factors. The first concerns the particular nature of the ethnographic method that is used by many anthropologists. The second has to do with the fact that theory of mind hovers somewhere on the boundary between the explicit and the implicit, the conscious and the subconscious, the objective and the subjective.

Much of the ethnographic evidence for culturally relative "theory of mind" is based on proverb-like statements, standardized declarations that people give in reply to predictable questions. In reality, these propositions are often meta-statements, intentionally paradoxical, ideological or poetical in nature, which rely for their sense on a shared but unspoken cognitive base. An analogy might be when a

Christian affirms that there is life after death, by which, of course, as most listeners know, she is not affirming that there is no difference between a noisy neighbor and a corpse (cf. Astuti et al. 2004).

In the writing of ethnography, however, these second-degree statements are often treated as if they were straightforward first-degree propositions that will provide access to the very foundations of the knowledge of the people who utter them. I would argue that the majority of the representations of the concepts of person, of mind, or of social relation that we find reported in the ethnographic literature, and that Lillard uses to critique cognitive psychology on theory of mind, are of this kind (cf. Spiro 1993). If they have appeared to us strange and exotic, it is because they are essentially second-degree statements that have been mistaken by anthropologists for first-degree propositions.

By contrast, when the Malagasy villagers witnessed their children performing the false belief task and were asked to interpret the results, they found themselves in a novel situation in which they had to use their knowledge and inferential capacities in flexible and creative ways. The effort required to debate this unexpected phenomenon left no room for the second-order talk that predictable situations and ready-made discourse allow. What the Malagasy villagers said when confronted with the false belief task was reflective and discursive, and thus very different in character from the fixed and proverb-like statements we find in the classical ethnographies. Consequently, it is not surprising that the type of discourse they produced on this occasion is more comparable with the equally reflective and discursive propositions of the scientists.

But there is another explication for the proximity between the scientific discourse and that of the Malagasy villagers than questions of anthropological methodology alone. The apparent difference between western scientific discourse and the data reported by the anthropologists and cited by Lillard has also to do with the ontological status of the psychologists' own understanding of theory of mind. Cognitive psychologists typically proceed by conducting experiments that make human subjects perform some closely controlled activity without, however, it being openly acknowledged that these human subjects might have their own opinions of

.what is going on. Thus, in the case of the false belief task, psychologists interpret the results—their subjects' performance—as if these allowed them to penetrate the mysteries of the "theory of mind" held by their subjects, a theory of which these subjects are, however, assumed to be unaware. Often the style of these interpretations makes it seem that the human mind—in its continual reading of the minds of others—functions quite independently of any process of which the person themselves might be remotely conscious. Yet, even if some aspects of the operation of theory of mind are totally inaccessible to the conscious mind, there are also some good reasons to think (as I have argued in Chapter 1) that many aspects can cross the broad and murky divide into consciousness. Indeed, the very practice of psychologists shows that they implicitly make this assumption. Thus, in the course of their experiments, psychologists are keen to collect what they term "justifications" from their subjects. These so-called "justifications" are explanatory statements of the following type: "Mummy does not know that you put the pencils there and so she believes there are Smarties in the box." Psychologists are more than happy to use explanations provided by their subjects as evidence in support of their interpretations of the experimental data. This shows *both* that we are not in fact dealing with a straightforward "subconscious" phenomenon, *and* that ordinary people's own understanding of theory of mind and the "theoretical" propositions of the psychologists are much more closely related than the way the scientists report the experimental data generally makes them appear.

To summarize the argument so far: There are two reasons why my research in Madagascar, instead of throwing up yet another account of some strange, exotic meta-theory of mind, produced an account of a meta-theory that is very similar to that elaborated by professional cognitive psychologists. The first reason is that unlike the anthropologists whose work Lillard uses to critique cognitive psychology, I adopted a methodology that provokes informants to formulate first-degree propositions. The second reason is that, despite the manner in which psychologists often represent the relation between their data and their theory, ordinary people can and do have conscious access to at least some of the workings of their theory of mind. To the extent that this is the case their meta-theory will necessarily reflect some of the same universal aspects that are theorized by psychologists. Their meta-theory is an interpretation of the same empirical phenomena that preoccupy psychologists.

Now the claim that Malagasy villagers reach similar conclusions about theory of mind to those of professional psychologists raises an even more fundamental question. How might this be possible when one would have supposed that Malagasy villagers, going about their daily business, and professional researchers, experimenting in their laboratories, were engaged in totally different activities? It is this question that I shall attempt to answer next.

Conducting the false belief task in the field has shown that Malagasy villagers are also capable, with minimal encouragement, of becoming theoreticians of the mind. No doubt, interpreting the results of the false belief task was an unusual activity for them and probably struck them as a little bizarre; but this does not mean that the theoretical reflection it required was completely new to them. In fact, both the ease with which these Malagasy villagers engaged in discussion of the experiment, as well as much of what they said, indicates that only the manner of the experiment was unusual. The fundamental questions it raised were ones that villagers had already thought about, and very likely had even debated among themselves.

There is a tendency in anthropology to believe that ordinary people's theoretical knowledge is inextricably embedded in practice, while that of scientists is more abstract and context-free. The type of fieldwork data I have just reported suggests that such a radical opposition is false. Ordinary life, even of virtually unschooled people, also allows for pure scientific speculation—science for the pleasure of understanding. For these Malagasy villagers living in remote forests, as indeed for us, life itself oscillates continually between practice and theory. Practice implies theoretical reflection, and theory is used to explore the implications of practice. All I did by introducing the false belief task was to create a novel trigger for villagers to engage in the kind of theoretical speculation that they would regularly initiate anyway in the course of everyday life. In short, scientists, in this case psychologists, and Malagasy peasants often engage in the same kind of activity. This above all is what explains why they offer similar theoretical interpretations of the false belief task.

Stressing the continuity of intellectual enterprise between professional scientists and those we study is not original. This point has already been argued by Claude Lévi-Strauss (1962), although he envisages the continuity in a less direct way than I am proposing here. For Lévi-Strauss, our science is another means of doing the kind of intellectual work that the Amerindians, in their way, accomplish through their myths. I would rather argue that, at least in the case of the Malagasy villagers described in this lecture, their mythology is like our mythology *while it is their science that resembles our own.* By science, I simply mean the continual effort to understand the world as it is by abstracting theory from practice. And if, as has been argued by some of the authors cited in this lecture, the distinctive feature shared by all human beings, and what renders human cognition unique, is above all our capacity, partly conscious, to interpret the mind of others so as to be able to live in extremely complex societies, it should not be so surprising that it is in this domain particularly that the reflections of the villagers and those of the scientists meet.

Ethnography and Theory

So, what does all this mean for the role of the anthropologist? I began this lecture by evoking the progressive disengagement of two wings of a discipline, torn between detailed ethnography and generalizing theory. Yet the chief protagonists in my story thus far have been Malagasy villagers and cognitive psychologists, while the anthropologists, whose legitimacy I was promising to rescue, seem to have disappeared. I want now to redress this imbalance by suggesting that it is the fact that Malagasy villagers and professional academics are *not* engaged in altogether different undertakings but rather share a compatibility of purpose that justifies the bifurcated practice of traditional anthropology and makes it so valuable. For it is precisely the common ground between the anthropologist and the people he or she studies that highlights the weaknesses of ethnography without theory and of theory without ethnography.

Even if the current trend is for ethnography for its own sake, bereft of generalizing theory, to become the dominant practice in anthropology departments around the world, the limitations of such a development are very clear. First of all, from a strictly methodological perspective, anthropologists can no longer justify their existence by claiming a monopoly in matters of knowledge of local realities. Formerly the ethnographer's raison d'être, the skills required are now exercised with equal competency by other social scientists: historians, geographers, area studies specialists, and especially local scholars who generally have the considerable advantage of being native speakers of the local language. Second, the limitations of pure ethnography are also of an epistemological order. Because the practice of ethnography without theory has no framework in which to place its data, it always runs the risk of becoming little more than a ragbag of anecdotes. Not only does this invite the "so what?" comment; it also leads the ethnographer to misrepresent the data he or she collects. This is because ethnography without theory slips, easily and surreptitiously, into reporting the representations of the peoples studied as if their lives were turned inward to a wholly self-referential, culturally constructed universe, and not also oriented toward a relation with the real world—a world that includes their bodies, including their own minds. The Malagasy villagers I have told you about are not trapped within hermeneutic circles. On the contrary, as we have seen, they are engaged in trying to understand and interpret the functioning of the human mind, their own and others," as it really is. Thus, the anthropologist is obliged to engage with theory if only to take full cognizance of, and to respond meaningfully to, the interests and concerns of the men and women he or she is studying.

On the other hand, theory that is not continually brought to heel by ethnography is also dangerous. For if the strengths of the scientific approach in terms of accuracy and rigor are obvious and well-known, it is also worth considering its drawbacks. *Theory,* as I understand the term here, consists in the formulation of general hypotheses about the nature of human beings on the basis of clarified empirical data. The production of such data in psychology involves all kinds of efforts to isolate, as far as possible, facts about the human psyche from the diverse circumstances in which they naturally occur. Producing theory, therefore, is a matter of presenting hypotheses as "cleanly" as possible. Inevitably, this involves a process of decontextualization both in the course of data collection and at the moment of formulating general propositions. For example, the performance of the standardized false belief task, as it is carried out in the laboratory, conventionally requires the random selection of subjects and the presentation of experimental stimuli under tightly controlled conditions, the expressed aim being to eliminate any factor that might distract the participants or influence their judgments. The reported findings of scientists are therefore dependent on an intentionally rarefied atmosphere and should be judged in this light.

Such simplification and purification can be taken even further. The philosophers' thought experiment is in many ways the extreme form of this process. It is not so different from the treatment of empirical data by the natural sciences, except that in this case the empirical is entirely replaced by the hypothetical so that reason can exercise its scrutiny in detached calm. Indeed, one famous definition of philosophy is that it is simply a matter of thinking slowly.

It clearly would be absurd not to acknowledge the value of the classical scientific method or of the conceptual analysis of philosophy. Both are tacks that have enabled us, and will continue to enable us, to make progress in all sciences, including those dealing with culture and society. Nonetheless, to continue the nautical theme, these tacks may be taken so tightly that they fail to make us advance at all or, dropping the nautical metaphor, cause us to lose sight of our ultimate objective, which is to understand the world as it really is. I would venture to say this: One can think so slowly and so cleanly that one erases the very phenomena one wanted to think about.

When it comes to studying human beings, what might be lost through the purifying procedures of science and philosophy is the fundamental fact that human beings, as we find them, exist only as social and historical beings, and that complexity and disorder are what characterize them and the world they inhabit. I have already noted with respect to "theory of mind" the extraordinary speed and complexity of thought that social life and culture require of us. Methodologies predicated on simplification and slow reflection by definition exclude these complex but essential aspects of reality from scrutiny. They "throw out the baby with the bath water," to employ a colloquial turn of phrase. To be sure, certain theoretical psychologists, notably Gibson and Neisser, are well aware of this danger, and have called for what they refer to as an "ecological approach." However, the elements of life in the real world that they have been able to incorporate into their experiments and their theoretical models will seem ridiculously inadequate to any anthropologist accustomed to conducting fieldwork. The desire for precision and rigor in the sciences often leads to the assumption that to study human nature one needs to strip human beings of their historical and cultural clothing. But the naked creatures that result are, very simply, no longer human beings. A cognitive anthropology grounded in fieldwork offers a sobering and necessary corrective to such an approach.

Conclusion

It is because I have become increasingly aware of the twin dangers of ethnography without theory and of theory devoid of empirical moorings that I maintain that it is the singular combination of both activities that enables anthropology to bring something of special value to the human sciences in general. It is not a matter of trying to obtain a perfect alloy of ethnography and theory. In my opinion, such an objective is out of reach. Rather it is a matter of keeping both tasks on the go and of moving between the two. Such a dual practice is admittedly hardly easy, but it is these constant comings and goings between ethnography and theory that confer on anthropology its unique character and explain the important contributions this discipline has made to knowledge in the past. I am not even sure that without its two-sided practice there would be much point in continuing the academic tradition that goes by the name of "anthropology." Theory draws us forward, but often so far and so fast that it takes us into a world in which the individual members of our species and the social world that characterize us can appear irrelevant and absent. Ethnography *without* some general theory, on the other hand, slows us down, ultimately to the point of immobility, by complicating things infinitely.

In any case, another element warns us against the temptation of ethnography for its own sake. The very people we study, such as the Malagasy villagers I have talked about in this lecture, and ultimately people everywhere, beckon us to return to the universe of theory. For the possibility of generalizing about human beings is certainly what interests them and about which they question us. As we have seen, Malagasy villagers tell us that if older children "pass" the false belief task, it is because they have learned to appreciate that people act in terms of what they believe to be true about the world rather than in terms of how the world is. But this is not all they say on the matter. They *go further* than the scientists and tell us that the child uses this knowledge in order to lie, to "do *politique*," to manipulate others; and, moreover, that this is a critical, perhaps fundamental, dimension of social life.

Just as these Malagasy villagers were in their own way endeavoring to negotiate the difficult terrain that lies between ethnography and theory, in my opinion anthropologists should follow suit, thereby maintaining the constant "to-ings" and "fro-ings" between the two kinds of research activity that characterized the discipline in the past. For me, an anthropologist in the true sense of the word is someone who, upon hearing a scientist propose some new general theory, does not dismiss it with ill-informed disdain, as happens all too often at present, but rather takes the trouble to consider how this theory might apply in the faraway place he or she has studied, but which the scientist proposing the theory is most unlikely to have had the occasion to know. Conversely, when an anthropologist becomes captivated by some aspect of local culture, an exotic ritual, for example, instead of succumbing to the specific detail of a strictly local perspective, he or she has the broader duty to ask why it is that given what we know about human beings in general, such phenomena occur. The continued vitality of anthropology, and of its distinctive gift to the study of humankind, depends on maintaining this tense but highly fertile to-and-fro motion between theory and ethnography, such as I have outlined here for "theory of mind." It is to these characteristic comings and goings between general theoretical considerations, too rapidly evoked, and specific ethnographic facts, so briefly described, that I shall be devoting future lectures and seminars.[1]

Note

1. I would particularly like to thank Rita Astuti and Paul Harris for their comments on the first draft of this text.

References

Astuti, R., G. Solomon, and S. Carey. 2004. Constraints on conceptual development: A case study of the acquisition of folkbiological and folksociological knowledge in Madagascar. *Monographs of the Society for Research in Child Development* 69, vii–135.

Avis, J., and P. L. Harris. 1991. Belief-desire reasoning among Baka children: Evidence for a universal conception of mind. *Child Development* 62, 460–467.

Baron-Cohen, S. 2000. Theory of mind and autism: A 15 year review. In *Understanding other minds: Perspectives from developmental cognitive neuroscience* (eds) S. Baron-Cohen, H. Tager-Flusberg, and D. J. Cohen, 3–21. Oxford: Oxford University Press.

Bloch, M. 1992. What goes without saying: The conceptualisation of Zafimaniry society. In *Conceptualising society* (ed) A. Kuper, 127–147. London: Routledge.

———. 1998. Autobiographical memory and the historical memory of the more distant past. In *How we think they think: Anthropological approaches to cognition, memory, and literacy* (ed) M. Bloch, 114–127. Boulder, CO: Westview Press.

———. 2004. Ritual and deference. In *Ritual and memory: Toward a comparative anthropology of religion* (eds) H. Whitehouse and J. Laidlaw, 65–78. Walnut Creek, CA: Altamira Press.

Callaghan, T., P. Rochat, A. Lillard, M. L. Claux, H. Odden, S. Itakura, S. Tapanya, and S. Singh. 2005. Synchrony in the onset of mental-state reasoning: Evidence from five cultures. *Psychological Science* 16(5), 378–384.

Carpenter, M., N. Akhtar, and M. Tomasello. 1998. Fourteen through eighteen month old infants differentially imitate intentional and accidental actions. *Infant Behavior and Development* 21, 315–330.

Dumont, L. 1966. *Homo hierarchicus: le système des castes et ses implications.* Paris: Gallimard.

Dunbar, R. 1992. Neocortex size as a constraint on group size in primates. *Journal of Human Evolution* 20, 469–493.

Frith, U., and C. Frith. 2001. The biological basis of social interaction. *Current Directions in Psychological Science* 10, 151–155.

Gergely, G., Z. Nadasdy, G. Csibra, and S. Biro. 1995. Taking the intentional stance at 12 months of age. *Cognition* 56, 165–193.

Harris, P. L. 2000. *The work of the imagination.* Oxford: Blackwell.

Humphrey, N. 1976. The social function of intellect. In *Growing points in ethology,* (eds) P. P. G. Bateson and R. A. Hinde, 303–317. Cambridge: Cambridge University Press.

Lévi-Strauss, C. 1962. *La pensée sauvage.* Paris. Plon.

Lillard, A. S. 1998. Ethnopsychologies: Cultural variations in theory of mind. *Psychological Bulletin* 123, 3–33.

Mauss, M. 1938. Une catégorie de l'esprit humain: La notion de personne, celle de "moi." *Journal of the Royal Anthropological Institute* 68, 263–281.

Poole, F. J. P. 1985. Coming into being: Cultural images of infants in Bimin-Kuskusmin folk psychology. In *Person, self and experience* (eds) G. M. White and J. Kirkpatrick, 183–244. Berkeley: University of California Press.

Scholl, B. J., and A. M. Leslie. 1999. Modularity, development, and "theory of mind." *Mind and Language* 14, 131–153.

Sperber, D. 2000. Metarepresentations in an evolutionary perspective. In *Metarepresentations: A multidisciplinary perspective* (ed) D. Sperber, 117–137. Oxford: Oxford University Press.

Spiro, M. 1993. Is the Western conception of the self "peculiar" within the context of the world cultures? *Ethnos* 21(2), 107–153.

Vinden, P. G. 1999. Children's understanding of mind and emotion: A multi-culture study. *Cognition and Emotion* 13(1), 19–30.

Wellman, H. 1998. Culture, variation and levels of analysis in folk psychologies: Comment on Lillard (1998). *Psychological Bulletin* 123, 33–36.

Wimmer, H., and J. Permer. 1983. Beliefs about beliefs. *Cognition* 13: 103–128.

◇

8

Lévi-Strauss as an Evolutionary Anthropologist

This chapter is the text of a lecture given in India as part of a celebration of Claude Lévi-Strauss's one-hundredth birthday. The lecture was addressed to a general academic audience, many of whom were anthropologists or sociologists, though from very different scholarly traditions. I wanted to combat certain hostile misconceptions that I believe are common in the English-speaking university world. I took the occasion to step back and to think about Lévi-Strauss's work as though I had just come to it for the first time and to reflect on his contribution in the most fundamental and general way possible.

The first thing to say about Lévi-Strauss is that he is an *anthropologist*. This was the self-designation that he chose on his return to France after World War II. He might have chosen another term, such as *sociologist* or *ethnologist*, terms which would have associated him with older, more established French traditions, but he chose to align himself with anthropology. Such words do not indicate distinct subject matters; they point to distinct academic traditions. Thus, it is not surprising that, for example, they mean somewhat different things in U.S. English, UK English, and Indian English. In the French context, Lévi-Strauss's choice meant that he intended to place his work within the framework defined by the English-speaking founders of the subject, and this is how I see his work.

As an academic subject, anthropology developed in the latter part of the nineteenth century with the extraordinary ambition of being *the* science of humankind, a science that was therefore going to define what human nature was as opposed to the nature of other animals. This science would use whatever evidence was available from archaeology, palaeontology, human biology, linguistics, and for cultural and social variation among contemporary human societies to understand fundamental questions concerning humankind.

In France in the middle of the twentieth century, Lévi-Strauss's choice of being an anthropologist, in what can be called the "strong" sense of the word, was an anomaly, especially for someone working in the field that has been roughly covered by social and cultural anthropology. This is so all the more because for the early anthropologists anthropology meant studying human evolution. We have learned much more than is usually acknowledged from these early anthropologists who founded the subject in the late nineteenth century; I believe these are the writers Lévi-Strauss resembles. But they got an awful lot wrong, and the main thrust of twentieth-century anthropology has been concerned with refuting their theories. Perhaps because of this, perhaps because of other reasons, the subsequent history of anthropology has been almost entirely negative: a history of retreat. Although we have accumulated a great deal of data in all the fields from which the early anthropologists sought evidence, the fundamental theoretical ambition of the subject has never stopped shrinking so that finally, in the last part of the twentieth century, we arrived at a stage when it was possible for a group of scholars to claim, as their greatest theoretical glory, to have no theory at all.

Against this defeatist background, the work of Lévi-Strauss stands in sharp contrast. He has always remained an anthropologist in the original sense of the word. He has maintained the definition of the subject as its nineteenth-century founders understood it. And he has done this while at the same time criticizing in the most fundamental way possible the assumptions that lay behind the most familiar evolutionary theories of the past or present. As we shall see, the basis of his criticism is that the early evolutionary writers had ignored the most evident evolutionary fact about *Homo sapiens*, the implications of the kind of mind evolution has created for the species.

When I consider Lévi-Strauss's contribution with "a view from afar," to use the title of one of his books, it is clear to me that throughout his work he has been proposing a coherent theory about the evolution of humankind and about human nature that is just as bold as any proposed by the founders of the discipline. I want to lay bare this general theory in this lecture. This, however, requires a certain amount of distancing from Lévi-Strauss's texts for a number of reasons. One is because other anthropologists, deep in their retreat mode, have almost wilfully ignored his most fundamental propositions and refused to discuss them so that they have fallen into the background. This is true even for his later work. Another is due to the character of the man himself, a characteristic shyness, that is best captured by that untranslatable French word *pudeur,* has made him hide his boldest claims a little and leave them undeveloped as though he was subsequently ashamed to have been so daring.

Because I have no such inhibitions, I shall attempt to expose the evolutionary perspective that lies behind his work in a way that he might well consider vulgar. I believe that this basic theoretical orientation has held steady throughout his work in spite of a change in emphasis.

What do I mean by "evolutionary" here? If we ignore certain aspects of his earlier publications, Lévi-Strauss's work implies the usual rejection of the nineteenth-century idea that different contemporary people around the world somehow represent different stages in the history of humankind. All living human beings are obviously equally distant from the first humans. What interests him is the variety of people around the world. This observation, however, is not made simply in order to marvel at cultural and social diversity but also to be used as a tool to understand the nature of human beings. Lévi-Strauss wants to understand human beings and that means understanding what their evolutionary history means for the way they are. What I mean by Lévi-Strauss being an evolutionist is therefore the same as what he himself meant by being an anthropologist. He is seeking a naturalist account of humankind, but not one that uses naturalism as an excuse for bypassing human specificity.

I start by offering an unorthodox interpretation of his first major work, published in 1949, significantly four years after the defeat of Nazi Germany: *The Elementary Structures of Kinship.*

I propose that this book contains a reflection on and a rejection of a particular take on human nature that we would now call sociobiology but that was already discernible at the time it was written and before in the precursor of sociobiology: eugenics. This theory was derived from the union of Darwinian natural selection with genetics and had been applied to humans and kinship. Putting it simply, the synthesis implied that the most successful individuals were those who produced the greatest number of viable offspring. This evolutionary fact was then used by some to explain the anthropological finding that in all human societies the mutual bonds uniting kinsmen are strong. According to some, this was because these kinship ties were derived from the genetic link between parents and children, and the parents' evolutionary interest in spreading their genes. Coupled with the then-common assumption that early societies were kinship-based, this was interpreted to mean that the urge to further one's bloodline against that of others was the natural and inevitable basis of society. The political overtone of such a reading of eugenics, not the only one by a long way, was that it became associated with the worst forms of racism.

In *The Elementary Structures of Kinship,* Lévi-Strauss maintains that a view that reduces human society to "blood ties" and to the selfish motivation of maintaining them misses the very essence of what it is to be human. If we use the perhaps unfortunate terminology that he chose, we can say that this eugenics-derived view of humans misses the fact that humans have passed "from nature to culture"; in other words, human society is quite different from that of other animals because it is based on conscious contract, not on blood ties. This emphasis on contract as the defining factor in human evolution inevitably leads to a consideration of the characteristics of the human mind that can create such a different kind of evolutionary history to that normally envisaged. This double emphasis on contract and the human mind is the basis of Lévi-Strauss's evolutionary theory. To argue such a key role for the rejection of eugenics in the development of Lévi-Strauss's theory may seem odd because the words *eugenics* or *Nazism* are never mentioned in *The Elementary Structures of Kinship,* as far as I know. But these omissions are in themselves a little odd given the time when Lévi-Strauss was developing his theory. I propose that eugenics and Nazism are the elephants in the room. However, I do not want to argue that the rejection of Nazi ideas is in any way an explanation of Lévi-Strauss's theory; instead, the former was a tool that enabled him to construct his theory.

The starting point of *The Elementary Structures of Kinship* is a consideration of rules prohibiting incest and the consequent central place of the obligation to reciprocate. For Lévi-Strauss these universal rules, which take a variety of forms, have the effect that human society cannot be based on blood ties, but that people through their intellect create complex systems of exchange or contract with genealogically unrelated people.

The ontological status of incest and reciprocity in Lévi-Strauss's work is ambiguous. In the case of incest, he seems to want to deny any instinctive grounding, whereas he pushes for such a basis in the case of reciprocity. However, the main point lies elsewhere: It is that the combination of the incest taboo and the reciprocity instinct are merely tools that can be used in the creation of an infinite variety of social systems. Thus the main body of the book illustrates by means of numerous ethnographic examples that first, the incest taboo requires out-marriage; and second, because of the human reciprocity instinct, this need to marry out leads to the definition of groups and roles that become ever more complex and the basis of social classifications. It is in terms of these classificatory systems that society is possible. These creations, which are the social systems we know, are thus the product of the activity of human minds. However, we must remember what has made it possible to create them: the kind of evolved brain that makes the shape of our head so different from that of chimpanzees. This cannot account for them, however, any more than a Louis XVI chest of drawers is explained by the toolbox of the cabinetmaker. We should beware of falling into the same error as sociobiologists of the time. Human social systems cannot be explained by a natural drive to look after blood relatives. Yet the natural basis of human social systems should never be overlooked.

I am suggesting that the emphasis on alliance-based kinship systems, which characterizes *The Elementary Structures of Kinship,* an emphasis that has fascinated and puzzled many anthropologists in equal measure, is not simply a technical matter but is an aspect of the demonstration of a fundamental theory about human evolution, albeit one that is also a criticism of the type of anthropological evolutionism that had been prevalent. What is being said is that because humans have brains that enable them to pass on ideas, one to another and across the generations, they are caught in systems of their own creation; they are caught in human history that is quite different from the natural history of species that do not have this brain specialization.

Putting the matter like this makes Lévi-Strauss's theory seem very similar to the Boasian anthropological theories to which he had been exposed and that he had, to a certain extent, admired during his stay in the United States during the war. However, I believe the similarity is limited. The anti-evolutionism of the American Boasians was total in most cases. What such Boasians as Margaret Mead, Ruth Benedict, and Alfred Kroeber were arguing was that because humans were cultural beings we could simply forget about the influence of biology and therefore about evolution. Culture made humans "super-organic," to use Kroeber's term. This is not Lévi-Strauss's position.

It is important to reflect on the fundamental difference in the understanding of what is meant by the word *culture* in his work and in that of the Boasian cultural anthropologists. For the latter, culture is the system through which we understand the world; it therefore exists before any thought or action can take place. It is a kind of cage within which we live and of whose existence we are unaware because we can only be *within* it. By contrast, for Lévi-Strauss culture is a continuous *process* of both reproduction and transformation.

It is a process that takes place in human minds. If we remember the famous quotation that Geertz borrows from Weber—that Man is an animal suspended in webs of meaning that he himself has spun—we find that Boasians, and Geertz himself, concentrate on the suspension while Lévi-Strauss concentrates on the spinning. As a result, it is inevitable that, unlike the Boasians, Lévi-Strauss insists that we pay attention to the mental action such an activity requires. We must consider the workings of the brain.

This is what explains the connection between the earlier book on kinship and what is probably Lévi-Strauss's most famous work, among anthropologists at least, *The Savage Mind*. In *The Elementary Structures of Kinship*, he emphasized how human culture is different from the culture of other living things, both in form and in kind, because of a natural evolved characteristic of *Homo sapiens*: the mind.

The Savage Mind is reminiscent of the earlier book in that it involves a similar feat of equilibrium. It argues for the relevance of the neurological workings of the evolved human brain for understanding the kinds of topics that have always concerned social and cultural anthropologists, but it also implies a fundamental criticism of those scientists who see in its working a *direct* explanation of human society and culture.

Lévi-Strauss's argument for the relevance to anthropology of scientific studies on the working of the mind is straightforward and had already been explicated unambiguously in a number of his earlier writings.

In order to inform himself about these disciplines, Lévi-Strauss had quite naturally turned to various cognitive sciences including psychology, neurology, artificial intelligence, and cognitive linguistics in much the same way as he had turned toward developmental psychology and primatology in order to understand reciprocity when writing *The Elementary Structures of Kinship*. Someone like Kroeber would never have done such a thing.

The image that Lévi-Strauss obtains from his study of these subjects is of a mind that resembles somewhat a Turing machine. Nowadays, of course, given the advances that have been made in our understanding of the working of the brain, his image is somewhat old-fashioned, but it was very sophisticated for its time, especially when compared to the simple stimulus/response psychology of behaviorism that was then predominant.

Interestingly, his psychological theory resembles in a number of ways the theories that the Swiss psychologist Piaget was in the process of developing at the time. This is because Lévi-Straussian "structure" resembles Piagetian "equilibration." This is so, even though Lévi-Strauss seldom refers to Piaget's work.

What makes the comparison with Piaget particularly interesting, however, is not just the points of similitude but also the fundamental differences. It is not difficult to imagine the twin related criticism Lévi-Strauss would make of the Piagetian approach. Piaget never seriously takes into account the fact that the child lives situated within a social world nor the fact that the world in which the child grows up, whether it be the material world, or the people with whom the child interacts, is already culturally structured. The Piagetian child has often been characterized as a lone scientist. She observes the world through her perceptive capacities and then makes sense of it, as though by herself. If Lévi-Strauss had thought about the growing child, a subject that as far as I know he has never written about, he would have emphasized how the material world in which the child develops is the product of the actions of other human beings who have made this world according to their aesthetic, practical, and ethical conceptions. And, furthermore, the people who made it would have done so in terms of the concepts of those who in turn surrounded them as children or adults. The people who surround the child are similarly the product of other people, and so on through the flow of history. The relation to the world available to perception is thus always, to a lesser or greater extent, mediated by culture. In other words, the child is always in the midst of the flow of history. It thus becomes rhetorically possible for Lévi-Strauss to assert that there is a sense in which, instead of allowing our theoretical imagination to concentrate on the image of individual people thinking myths, we can also imagine the myths living through and via people.

This emphasis on people being always situated within the flow of culture is the source of the originality of Lévi-Strauss's psychological theory. In contrast to the Boasians, he insists on our thinking of culture as a process in which individuals are actively involved, but he also insists that the individual mental process occurs within processes that transcend the individual. The analysis of a process within processes is captured by one of his most productive ideas, an idea that he indicates by the word *transformation.*

It is true that in Lévi-Strauss's work transformations are described in a rather mechanical way in terms of inversions, nesting, and so on. This is misleading and not in accord with what we now know. Nonetheless, the proposition at the core of his idea of transformation is most valuable. It is that culture at every stage involves reinvention and re-creation, rather than mere transmission.

Every individual receives and re-creates. Even if that individual reproduces exactly what he or she has received, this is just as much an act of creation as when he or she modifies it. Culture is thus a multitude of acts of individual cognitive creation of material that is already there but within an endless process of creation.

Here I want to emphasize two interesting implications that flow from this way of seeing things. The first is that the image of "bounded cultures," a representation that necessarily follows from the view of culture as a framework within which action and thought take place, becomes unacceptable. The cultural process has no boundary; any interruption in communication between neighbors can only be temporary. Furthermore, it is not simply that cultures flow into each other without any real boundaries; it is that the gradients that can be established for any particular item do not map one on another. If we take the example of myth, which Lévi-Strauss made the subject of the massive four-volume study usually referred to by their French title *Mythologiques*, we find that the myths known by an individual link up each with others in quite different directions. Thus it is not only that there are no boundaries; it is that there is no possible localization of the cultures, either in term of groups or even of gradients. This is a phenomenon that some sociologists seem to believe has occurred only in the modern world. Yet, for Lévi-Strauss, it is just as characteristic of the pre-contact Amerindian world. It is a situation that has always existed in the history of humankind.

The other implication of the notion of transformation concerns the nature of this cultural material that is being continually reinvented. If we recall for an instant the developmental story outlined by Piaget, we would imagine the child first perceiving the world and then deducing from its observations general abstract principles that would form the basis of ever more general theories. This story resembles the traditional view of the scientific method. Lévi-Strauss would argue that the story is mistaken; the child does not develop from a precultural state to a cultural state. The child is in a cultural world from the very beginning and thinks with already-made concepts about the real world. What we need to study is not, therefore, the evolution of a mind that would be adapted to operate from a zero cognitive starting point but the evolution of a mind adapted to operate *within* the flow of history. I believe that this is what Lévi-Strauss is struggling to define in *The Savage Mind*, though I do not think he gets much further than specifying the kinds of considerations that need to be taken into account in approaching the question. In defining the project, however, he has taken a major step.

In conclusion, let me return to the decision Lévi-Strauss made when he chose the term *anthropology* in the context of late 1940s France. It meant that he saw his own work as part of a science whose general enterprise was to understand the nature of human beings in a broad evolutionary framework. In pursuing this path, he went against the trend of the time, a trend that was moving toward the abandonment of this broad aim. Although Lévi-Strauss's work would take place principally within the subsection of anthropology that was called *cultural anthropology* in the United States and *social anthropology* in Britain, it would nonetheless retain the original ambition of anthropology as an integrated science. He was critical in a fundamental way of all the evolutionary anthropology that had gone before and that still survived in some quarters. He had no interest in the older evolutionary anthropology that spent its energy in placing different contemporary groups in a pseudohistorical ranking. He was rejecting models of human societies that forgot about the revolutionary implications of the human brain. Understanding this had to be made central to anthropology. However, the available work in psychology was also found wanting because it misrepresented people as outside the cultural historical process. His insistence on the crucial importance of ethnography is concerned to address this. The contribution of ethnography is to force the theoreticians to deal with the coal face of the unique specificity of actual human groups and their thought so that they come up with a theory that does not replace people as they live their lives within the cultural process with ciphers outside history, created by the psychological laboratory. Lévi-Strauss concentrates on Amerindians not only because he is attracted by their culture but also because they furnish an example of people with extremely low population densities who live in close interaction with other living species and thus give us an inkling of what the human condition has been for at least 99 percent of its history.

What we have therefore in the work of Lévi-Strauss is a study of the kind of people evolution has produced, and such a study has to be centrally concerned with the human mind because that is what distinguishes our species from other species. He therefore asks what have been the implications of this human mind for the natural history of the species. He has given an answer through the common device of criticizing the work of others, the early anthropologists, the American cultural anthropologists, and psychologists. These criticisms have been made, above all, in order to stress what their attempts to characterize human evolution have omitted: anthropology. In stressing how Lévi-Strauss's work has continued to be part of the general enterprise of *anthropology*, the term he chose for the personal chair he held at the Collège de France, I wanted to show how different his approach has been from the general drift of the subject during recent years. The recent history of anthropology has seen the abandonment of the big questions; the subject has often become little more than a parochial concern with the professional practice of anthropology rather than a deep engagement with its proper subject of study.

In staying true to the original calling of anthropology, Lévi-Strauss's work has been an oddity throughout the twentieth century and it remains an oddity today. A very wide range of different types of research is being undertaken under the label *cultural and social anthropology*, much of which is very valuable and serious, but the general fundamental anthropology that Lévi-Strauss carried on and forward throughout his long career is often missing.

Anthropology, in Lévi-Strauss's sense of the word, has continued but largely within other academic departments. It has carried on because the fundamental anthropological questions that the early anthropologists raised still fascinate all normal human beings, with the possible exception of those who are found in social and cultural anthropology departments. In a sense this does not matter. As mentioned previously, labels such as *anthropology, sociology, ethnology,* and so on are arbitrary. However, a problem does arise when biologists, neurologists, and even philosophers manifest their new enthusiasm for anthropology in the fundamental sense that Lévi-Strauss has understood it. This is because those working in biology, neurology, philosophy, and other such disciplines do not do what Lévi-Strauss stressed was necessary; they do not continually bruise their theories against the complexity and the variety of human cultures that the discipline of anthropology has been so good at bringing to the fore. Consequently, they run the risk of repeating all the old mistakes.

In my view, what is needed is the continuing presence in anthropology departments of anthropologists—that is, evolutionary anthropologists in the sense that Lévi-Strauss was. Not that this should be the only work that goes on in anthropology departments; it never has been. But it should remain a core pursuit; an attempt to answer the general questions about human beings to which people want answers, but to which they usually get the overly simple type of answers that Lévi-Strauss showed were misleading.

What is needed, therefore, is the renewal of the fruitful tension that is so central in his work between the complexity that comes from thinking about human beings in the context of the real histories and cultural flows in which they find themselves and the need to think in general terms about the kind of animal human beings are. Those who do this in anthropology departments today are rare, but it seems to me that very recently their numbers have begun to increase. Because of this, I am cautiously hopeful that Lévi-Strauss's work will not prove to be what it sometimes may appear—a grand immobile statue in a public park—but will resemble more the plants growing around such a statue that set and scatter their seeds as they pass.

◇

Index

of the state and, 31–36; imagination influencing the transcendental social, 37–38; individual and societal interpenetration, 18; lack of in chimpanzees, 25; neurological basis for, 23–25 ; science and, 109–110; transcendental social features, ix, 29–31. *See also* Christianity; Hinduism; Islam; Judaism; Mormons; Seventh Day Adventists

Renfrew, Colin, 23

Representations of the social, 126; anthropological theory, 115–117; linguistic communication, 8. *See also* Names; Transcendental social

Reproduction: house-based societies, 88–89. *See also* Children

Rituals: anthropological representation, 115–116; circumcision in the Merina Kingdom, 34; corporate groups and, 91–92; deference and, 17; interpenetration of individuals, 16–17; material objects as visible trace of, 92–93; naming children, 61–64; permanent names and transcendental roles, viii; rebounding violence, 95; relating sleep, death, and mind, 105–107; role in creating the transcendental social, vii, viii, ix, 91; transforming transactional social into transcendental social, viii; Zafimaniry death monuments, 71–72. *See also* Durkheim

Roles, social, viii, 90–92, 95. *See also* Transcendantal social

Rome, Imperial: political roots of religion, 35

Sacrifice, 95

"Sapient paradox", 23–24

The Savage Mind (Lévi-Strauss), 143–146

Science: religion and, 109–110; scientific speculation in ordinary life, 128–129

Scientific method, 131–132. *See also* Reasoning

Seeing. *See* Sight

Self, understandings of the, 120–122. *See also* Person

Semantics, 116–118

Semi-propositions, 109

Semiotic models, 57–58, 88

Senses: divination as truth-telling, 52; truth and, 41–43, 47–48, 51, 52, 54(n4); use in reasoning, 104

Seventh Day Adventists, 109–110

Sex and birth, 3–5, 10, 16

Shadow states, 34

Shared doubt, 100–101, 103–105, 108–110

Shared thought, 104–105

Sight, ix; truth and, 41–43, 47–48, 52, 54(n4); use in reasoning, 104

Sleep, mind in, 105–108

Smith, Joseph, 36

Sociability: as innate human capacity, 10; cognitive capacity as source of, 19; deceit and, 49; false belief task, 45; *Homo sapiens* and other primates, 6–7, 28; individual boundaries, 9–10; theory of mind and, 10;

theory and psychological
theory, 125; subconscious-
conscious interpenetration,
12–13; trust, 9. *See also*
Interpenetration; Mind
reading; Mutual monitoring
Thought: deceit and, 45–48;
dreams, 13–14; false belief
task explaining the nature
of, 11–12
Thucydides, 41
Time: defiance of, viii,
70, 82–83, 90, 93, 95;
transcendental social, 91
TOM, see Theory of mind
Tombs, 59, 71–72, 85
Touch: sight and, 42–43
Transactional social: as
evolutionary social force,
vii; as common to all
social species, vii; pre-
sapiens ancestors of
modern humans and, vii;
house-based societies,
90–93; social organization
in chimpanzees and
humans, 26; transcendental
networks and individual
boundaries, 29; relationship
to transcendental social,
viii, ix, 26–39. *See also*
Machiavellian social
Transcendental order, see
Transcendental social
Transcendental social: as
second-order phenomenon,
vii; as unique to *Homo
sapiens,* viii; as essentialized
roles and groups, vii, 26–29;
as transcendental roles
and groups, vii; house-
based societies, 90–95;
imagination influencing,
25, 36–38; neurological
basis for, 23–25; political

and religious development,
31–36; relationship to
transactional social, viii, ix,
25, 58; religion and, 29–31;
ritual and, vii; sociability
and, 30. *See also* Social;
Transactional social
Transformation: historical,
viii; of symbolical systems
of subjects, 33; of bodies
into houses, 60, 74; in
Lévi-Strauss's work, 142,
144–145. *See also* Social;
Transactional social
Trees, thought in, 103, 104
Trust, 9
Truth: divination as truth-
telling, 51–52; doubt and,
99–100; ethnography of,
ix–x, 51; false belief task,
44–48, 124–125; knowledge
through hearing and sight,
54(n4); language shaping the
social, 53; representational
role of names, 58; rhetorics
of, x; seeing and sight, ix,
41–43, 47–48

Upper Palaeolithic revolution:
development of imagination,
23, 37–38; origins of
religious-like beliefs, 25;
transcendental social, viii
Urban flight, 73–74

Villages: Çatalhöyük houses,
82–83; Zafimaniry houses,
84

Witchcraft, 16
World Heritage significance, 84

Zafimaniry people, ix;
baptismal names, 72–75;
Christianity, 72–73;

Earlier versions of the following chapters were previously published:

Chapter 1: Bloch, Maurice (2007) Durkheimian anthropology and religion: Going in
and out of each other's bodies. In: *Religion, anthropology, and cognitive science* (eds)
H. Whitehouse and J. Laidlaw, 63–80. North Carolina: Carolina Academic Press.

Chapter 2: Bloch, Maurice (2008) Why religion is nothing special but is central.
Philosophical transactions of the Royal Society B: biological sciences, 363 (1499),
2055–2061.

Chapter 3: Bloch, Maurice (2008) Truth and sight: Generalizing without
universalizing. *Journal of the Royal Anthropological Institute*, 14 (s1). S22–S32.

Chapter 4: Bloch, Maurice (2006) Teknonymy and the evocation of the "social"
among the Zafimaniry of Madagascar. In: *An anthropology of names and naming*
(eds) G. vom Bruck and B. Bodenhorn, 97–114. Cambridge: Cambridge University
Press.

Chapter 5: Bloch, Maurice (2010) Is there religion in Çatalhöyük . . . or just
houses? In: *Religion in the emergence of civilization: Çatalhöyük as a case study* (ed)
I. Hodder, 146–163. Cambridge: Cambridge University Press.

Chapter 7: Bloch, Maurice (2006) *L'anthropologie cognitive à l'épreuve du terrain*
(trans.). Paris: Fayard.

◇

About the Author

The distinguished anthropologist Maurice Bloch is Professor of Anthropology at the London School of Economics and
Political Science. His work is unique in that he is both an active field-working anthropologist and a general theoretician.
Bloch has been a leading figure among those anthropologists
who seek to reintegrate social and anthropological theory
with the work of cognitive scientists and prehistorians.